MW00622221

HOW
GREAT
IS OUR
GOD

HOW
GREAT
IS OUR
GOD

Living a Worship-Led Life
in a Me-Driven World

BY CHRIS TOMLIN
WITH J.D. WALT

K-LOVE
BOOKS

FRANKLIN, TENNESSEE

K-LOVE. BOOKS

5700 West Oaks Blvd.
Rocklin, CA 95765

Published by K-LOVE Books, an imprint of EMF Publishing, LLC, 5700 West Oaks Blvd., Rocklin, CA 95765.

K-LOVE Books/EMF Publishing is an imprint of Forefront Books. Distributed by Simon & Schuster.

Printed in the United States of America.

First edition: 2024
10 9 8 7 6 5 4 3 2 1

ISBN: 978-1-63763-312-0 (Hardcover)
ISBN: 978-1-63763-313-7 (E-book)

Library of Congress Control Number: 2024901173

DEDICATION

*I dedicate this book to my beautiful daughters . . .
Ashlyn, Madison and Elle . . . that some day these
words might inspire and remind you of why your
dad leaves the house with his guitar to inspire and
remind others . . . how great is our God.*

TABLE OF CONTENTS

OUTWARD

FOREWORD

by Max Lucado

I never grow weary of telling the story of a nine-year-old housebound boy who was diagnosed with a case of mononucleosis. The doctor ordered him to stay indoors for the entire summer. He was a rambunctious, athletic, outgoing kid. To be told he must spend a summer indoors? No Little League baseball, fishing trips, or bike rides? Might as well trap an eagle in a birdcage.

This was a nine-year-old's version of a tempest.

The boy's dad, however, was a man of faith. He resolved to find something good in the quarantine. He sold guitars in his drugstore and wasn't a half-bad guitarist himself. So he gave his son a guitar. Each morning the dad taught the boy a new chord or technique and told him to practice it all day. The youngster did. Turns out, the kid had a knack for playing the guitar. By the end of the summer, he was playing Willie Nelson tunes and beginning to write some songs of his own.

Within a few years he was leading worship in churches. Within a few decades he was regarded as the "most sung songwriter in the world."* Few among us haven't been blessed by his songs: "How Great Is Our God," "Whom Shall I Fear," "Our God."

Chris Tomlin has spent a lifetime teaching us to do what he learned to do that summer—exchange his misfortune for music. Under his direction, millions of us have lifted our eyes off of ourselves and our own version of summer setbacks and set our eyes on our Father and His heavenly goodness.

I think the world of Chris. It's an honor to call him a friend. We've traveled and ministered together on many occasions and in many places. He is a minstrel to our generation, reminding us that God is greater than any problem we face.

In this wonderful book, Chris does more than sing; he teaches. He shows us how to expand our view of God through worship. He calls us out of the me-driven world and into a worship-led life. As God grows larger, self and even our struggles seem smaller. You will find this volume to be full of insight, encouragement, and guidance. Chris bids us all to do what he learned to do as a youngster: focus less on our self-oriented pursuits and more on the greatness of God.

---

* "Chris Tomlin Most Sung Songwriter in the World," CBNNews .com, July 2, 2013, www.cbn.com/cbnnews/us/2013/july/chris -tomlin-most-sung-songwriter-in-the-world/?mobile=false.

I never endured what Chris did. I was never stuck indoors, but I was stuck in a storm. In the early pages of my childhood memory, I see this picture. My father and I were fishing. Small boat on a huge lake on a great day for catching bass. Out of nowhere a storm swooped down upon the water. In a matter of moments, the lake was white-topped and the boat was bouncing. Gray clouds billowed, lightning zigzagged, rain pelted the water surface and my ten-year-old heart bounced in my chest like sneakers in a clothes dryer. Fear had me in her talons. What other emotion could I feel? Every direction I looked was bad news. Look up and see the storm. Look down and see the waves. Look forward, I can't see the beach.

But then I looked back. I looked at my father. He was driving the boat. His face was calm. Soaked and dripping, but calm. Who knows why, but it was. With hand on the throttle, he resolutely motored the boat toward the shore.

At that moment I realized something. I could behold the storm and find fear or behold my father and find faith.

I chose my father's face.

So can we.

This life comes with storms. The presence of problems is inevitable. We cannot choose a storm-free life. But we can choose where to stare in the midst of one.

Thank you, Chris, for showing us how to look into the face of our Father.

INTRODUCTION

The scene stunned the watching world. Coco Gauff, the teenage tennis phenom, had just defeated her last opponent to win the US Open Tennis Championships. She fell to the ground in relief. After congratulating her opponent and hugging her parents, she made her way to the bench where she sat down and burst into uncontrollable crying. Her next move? She knelt in front of her bench, folded her hands, and began to pray. ESPN captured the image well but completely whiffed on the caption:

> @CocoGauff took a moment to soak it all in after winning her first grand slam title.

The celebrated football coach Tony Dungy couldn't let it stand. He wrote back:

> "I hate to break this to you SportsCenter but Coco Gauff was not 'soaking it all in' at this moment. She was praying. She has been very open about her Christian faith in the past. It seems obvious what she is doing here."

To make it abundantly clear, Gauff later said, "I don't pray for results. I just ask that I get the strength to give it my all. Whatever happens, happens. I'm so blessed in this life. I'm just thankful for this moment. I don't have any words for it, to be honest."

It is a picture of remarkable contrast. Coco Gauff, at the pinnacle of achievement in her career, pauses as though to say, "How great is our God," and the watching world suggests she is soaking it up in self-satisfaction. Gauff shows us a picture of a worship-led life in a me-driven world. That's the purpose of this book. It's what I have sought to make the purpose of my life: leading people to worship God.

Clearly, we are living in a me-driven age. Everyone clamors to build their personal security, to craft their own brand, to make a name for themselves. Meanwhile, there is only one name worthy of worship. His is the name above every name: Jesus. It's why I write songs. Just so we're clear, though, a worship-led life is not about songs and singing. That's why I'm writing this book. The songs are the soundtrack. The life is the story. In these pages I will share the wisdom I have gleaned and some of the stories behind some of the songs, but the point is to call and inspire you— not to merely sing the songs but to live the life.

From the earliest days of our fallen human race, we have sought glory for ourselves. From my earliest years, I have felt this me-driven spirit so strong around me, vying for my heart. At the same time, I was growing up in a family and in a church that were both pointing me to the greatness of God. Thank God His whisper is louder than the world's shout.

One afternoon I was sitting in my apartment in Austin, Texas, with my Bible open, reading Psalm 104. It's a beautiful song of praise that begins with this:

> LORD my God, you are very great; you are clothed
> with splendor and majesty. The Lord wraps himself in
> light as with a garment; he stretches out the heavens
> like a tent. (vv. 1–2)

The Psalm continues with several verses layering high praises that celebrate the greatness of God.

Songs are mysteries, and I still don't understand where they come from, but I remember grabbing my guitar one day when I read that psalm. And I began to sing out a simple chorus:

"How great is our God. Sing with me, how great is our God, and all will see how great is our God."

I remember thinking to myself, *This chorus is way too simple. It will never work.* Weeks later I began to frame the verses around that chorus as I went back to Psalm 104 for inspiration. I worked hard to keep every lyric pointed to the greatness of God, with nothing about me or you in there.

Songs about our human need for help and deliverance are good, and certainly the Bible is filled with them. The Bible is also filled with Scriptures and songs devoted exclusively to the glory of God. I call the former *songs of deliverance* and the latter *songs of transcendence.* I have noticed over the years that the church tends to sing more songs of deliverance than songs of transcendence. It's understandable, because we have such desperate need for God's help. Yet I have noticed something else over the years: every time, without fail, those songs of transcendence completely change the room. They take our eyes off of ourselves and our needy situations and put them on God alone.

The more conscious we become of the greatness of God, the more we lose sight of ourselves and all the complex challenges of our lives. When we enter into new depths of relationship with God, our perspective and posture toward our problems also change. Maybe it's why Jesus said things like this:

> "So do not worry, saying, 'What shall we eat?' or 'What shall we drink?' or 'What shall we wear?' For the pagans run after all these things, and your heavenly Father knows that you need them. But seek first his kingdom and his righteousness, and all these things will be given to you as well." Matthew 6:31–33

This is one of the biggest keys to the worship-led life: if we want to break free of me-driven living, we must begin with God, not ourselves. Even in our songs, we tend to start where we are—at our point of desperation and need. But when we begin with ourselves, we never quite get our focus on God. If we instead begin with God and bring our exclusive focus to His greatness and glory, we mysteriously find our challenging situations lightening up and even lifting off of us. When we seek Him first, He takes care of the rest. Songs of deliverance tend to naturally find their place and rise up in the wake of songs of transcendence.

This is the point of a worship-led life. We all come to the table broken and needy. That fact is inescapable. We are all sinners, which is to say we have a self-centered gravity.

A self-centered gravity leads to a me-driven world. In a me-driven world, everyone is desperately trying to orchestrate everything to solve their own problems and serve their own needs, interests, ambitions, agendas, projects, and so forth. The unintended result is that we try, with our worship, to bring God into our orbit—to enlist His movement to revolve around our activity (ironically, in His own name).

A worship-led life means living with a God-centered gravity—where we are the ones revolving our lives and everything in them around His reality. And isn't that the *ultimate* reality? All of reality centers on God, whether we know it or not, whether we realize it or not, and whether we want it to or not. A worship-led life is an ever-growing awakening to this truth. It is the massive movement from "I need you to help me, God," to "I want you to have me, God." We are so prone to seeking God's hand of help, and God is ever ready to help. What delights Him most, though, is when we start by seeking His face. After all, didn't Jesus say something like, "Your Father knows what you need before you ask Him"? I think you are getting the point.

The worship-led life unfolds a "movemental" life—a movement from *upward* to *inward* and then *outward*. To be sure, as we lift our lives to God our good, good Father, He comes powerfully into the deepest recesses of our innermost selves, where He transforms us into His likeness. That is the secret of the worship-led life: Jesus Christ, the worship leader, within us. From here our lives move outward and into the lives of others by the person and power of the Holy Spirit.

Let's look it at it through the lens of what Jesus called the greatest commandment. One day the religious authorities, to try and trip Jesus up, asked Him which was the greatest commandment in all of the Law. He swung for the fences:

> *"You shall love the Lord your God with all your heart and with all your soul and with all your strength and with all your mind, and your neighbor as yourself."*
> (Luke 10:27 ESV)

It is as though Jesus responded, "Hello Love!" Love God. Love Yourself. Love Others. That's the whole of the worship-led life, isn't it? Upward. Inward. Outward. I want you to see this little book as an invitation to a live a worship-led life—a life lifted upward and transcended by the holiness and goodness of God our Father, a life transformed inwardly by the indwelling Jesus Christ, and a life of imparting the love of God to others by the Holy Spirit.

That's my hope. I want to see many of you take your first steps into a worship-led life. I want to see many more of you take a deeper dive into a worship-led life. The me-driven life is tiring, uninteresting, and ultimately a waste of time. We all know where it leads: to a never-ending quest for more, which always turns out to be much less than we imagined. And aren't we more than a little bit tired of a "driven" life? Isn't it time we followed a better leader—one who doesn't drive but leads us into the glorious reality of the greatness of God?

Here's my counsel on how to proceed. I would love for you to carve out at least twenty-one minutes every day for the next twenty-one days. Ideally, that time will be first thing in the morning. Each day will guide you to read the reflection on the worship-led life. This will be followed by an element called *The Bridge*. In a song, we have the verses, the chorus, and then the bridge. The bridge is that part of the song which brings it all together and completes it. Finally, we will close each day with an element called *Sing With Me*. I'll suggest a song or two we can sing together to lead us out into the day. You can find the songs on our playlist at www.christomlin.com/singwithme, or cobble together a playlist on whatever platform you prefer. Even better, ask a friend to join you on the journey and compare notes along the way about how you are growing. I hope even whole churches might consider taking this journey of a worship-led life all together.

One more thing. These twenty-one reflections on the worship-led life will have two bookends. I want to open our journey together with an invitation you will find below— the doorway into the worship-led life. It is the story of how God came down to us, which is why we lift our hearts up to Him in the first place. Through the closing bookend we will look forward to the end of all things broken and the beginning of all things made new.

THE INVITATION

When I was growing up, every single week without fail, my small-town church would end the same way: with an altar call. The pastor would give "the invitation" to anyone and everyone to come just as they were to the altar to repent of their sins and accept Jesus Christ as their Lord and Savior. Then we would sing every verse of the classic hymn "Just as I Am" and wait to see who would come forward.

While I treasure these memories, I'd like to take a different approach. Rather than save it for the end, let's begin with the invitation. A worship-led life begins at the altar. I invite you to kneel with me at the altar and consider the invitation—to enter into a relationship with the God of the cosmos.

There's something we need to understand, though. It's the bad news: until we have received and responded to this invitation, we are outside of relationship with God. *How did this happen?* you may ask. *Doesn't God love everyone?* Absolutely. We need go no further than the most famous verse in the history of verses—John 3:16—to know this:

For God so loved the world that he gave his one and only Son, that whoever believes in him shall not perish but have eternal life.

So why did God have to give up His only son? In short, because our ancient ancestors, and every one of us since then, opted for the me-driven world. Open your Bible and scan the incredible gifts of Genesis chapters one and two and see how God provided every extravagance for those of us made in His very image. He gave us everything we would ever need to live the worship-led life:

Now the LORD God had planted a garden in the east, in Eden; and there he put the man he had formed. The LORD God made all kinds of trees grow out of the ground—trees that were pleasing to the eye and good for food. In the middle of the garden were the tree of life and the tree of the knowledge of good and evil.
Genesis 2:8–9

All the makings of the worship-led life were present from the very beginning. We were made to know and love God and to be known and loved by God. We were made to know and love each other and to be known and loved by each other. This is life in all its fullness. This is the worship-led life.

In the midst of this massive grant of provision came one simple warning:

The LORD God took the man and put him in the Garden of Eden to work it and take care of it. And the LORD God commanded the man, "You are free to eat from any tree in the garden; but you must not eat from the tree of the knowledge of good and evil, for when you eat from it you will certainly die." Genesis 2:15–17

Then watch what happened:

Now the serpent was more crafty than any of the wild animals the LORD God had made. He said to the woman, "Did God really say, 'You must not eat from any tree in the garden'?" Genesis 3:1

I want us to notice the deception here. God said we could eat from every tree in the garden but warned us about the one. Satan and evil work by distorting what God says in order to to deceive us. Deception paves the pathway into the me-driven world. Now, watch how deception works:

The woman said to the serpent, "We may eat fruit from the trees in the garden, but God did say, 'You must not eat fruit from the tree that is in the middle of the garden, and you must not touch it, or you will die.'" Genesis 3:2–3

Weren't there two trees in the middle of the garden? It makes me wonder if they stopped eating fruit from the Tree of Life. And what is this about "touching" the tree? Where did that come from? So much to ponder here. Watch how the deceiver takes this encounter to the next level:

"You will not certainly die," the serpent said to the woman. "For God knows that when you eat from it your eyes will be opened, and you will be like God, knowing good and evil." Genesis 3:4–5

There it is. The father of all lies gives them the ultimate deception behind all temptation: "You will be like God." We are created in the very image of God and yet still strive to be His equal. This is the me-driven world in a nutshell.

When the woman saw that the fruit of the tree was good for food and pleasing to the eye, and desirable for gaining wisdom, she took some and ate it. She also gave some to her husband, who was with her, and he ate it. Then the eyes of both of them were opened, and they realized they were naked; so they sewed fig leaves together and made coverings for themselves. Genesis 3:6-7

This is the origin story of how we exchanged the worship-led life for the me-driven world. What happens next holds three of the most beautiful words in all of Scripture:

Then the man and his wife heard the sound of the LORD God as he was walking in the garden in the cool of the day, and they hid from the LORD God among the trees of the garden. But the LORD God called to the man, "Where are you?" Genesis 3:8–9

Where are you?

God comes to us in the lost state of our wandering, somewhere between self-loathing and self-protection, in the cool of the day, pursuing us with the piercing question of grace: Where are you? Instead of scolding, He seeks us out. Instead of accusing, He comes asking: Where are you? Into our regret He comes to restore us into relationship.

We must come out of hiding and locate ourselves. Our forebears and all of us since entered into a cycle of shaming and blaming. Instead of humbly owning our lives, we proudly opted into the way of the me-driven world: self-justification.

Instead of death, God clothes us with garments of grace and grants us passage from the garden of His presence into the wilderness of the world.

Meanwhile, this story of the me-driven world doesn't stop. Soon thereafter, Adam and Eve's son Cain succumbs to the soul cancer of comparison. That leads to envy and a brewing rivalry with his brother, Abel, resulting in a fit of jealous rage that ends in murder. God asks Cain the ever-pressing question, "Where is your brother Abel?" (Genesis 4:9).

Where are you? Where is your brother? Where is your sister? Where is your neighbor?

In Genesis, we watch as the me-driven world comes to such compounded wickedness and complex brokenness that God determines to start over.

> *The LORD saw how great the wickedness of the human race had become on the earth, and that every inclination of the thoughts of the human heart was only evil all the time. The LORD regretted that he had made human beings on the earth, and his heart was deeply troubled.* Genesis 6:5–6

Our great God searches for someone, anyone, walking a worship-led life, and He finds Noah:

Noah was a righteous man, blameless among the peo-
ple of his time, and he walked faithfully with God.
Genesis 6:9

If you don't know the story from there, read it. Times
have changed, but people have not. Despite the massive
reset, this story of the me-driven world continues. We arrive
on the ancient plains of Shinar just as the people conspire to
overtake the heavens:

> *They said to each other, "Come, let's make bricks and*
> *bake them thoroughly." They used brick instead of*
> *stone, and tar for mortar. Then they said, "Come, let*
> *us build ourselves a city, with a tower that reaches to*
> *the heavens, so that we may make a name for our-*
> *selves; otherwise we will be scattered over the face of*
> *the whole earth."* Genesis 11:3–4

The ambitious agenda of the me-driven world could
not be more clear: *"so that we may make a name for our-*
selves." This story continues to the present moment. We all
find ourselves in some state of hiding from God. As we
hide from God, we become lost to ourselves. The first sign
we have become lost to ourselves is how we endlessly begin
comparing ourselves to others. The more we become lost to
ourselves, the more we become all about ourselves. After
all, in the me-driven world, the name of the game is the
game of the name—making a name for ourselves.

There is another name, though, a name that stands
above them all. It is the name of Jesus, the Son of God,
whom our Father would send into our sin-sick situation

to save us from the me-driven mess we have made of the world and restore us to the worship-led life for which we were made.

The name is Jesus.

Scripture calls Him the Second Adam—the one of whom it is said,

> He became sin, who knew no sin
> That we might become His righteousness
> He humbled Himself and carried the cross
> Love so amazing, love so amazing

The Bible uses a tiny yet massive word to capture all that is sick and broken about the me-driven world. That word is *sin*. Sin is the sickness infecting us all—the brokenness that has led us all to walk away from a worship-led life and become lost in a me-driven world. Sin is why we stand together at an altar with the Worship Leader, who is Jesus, considering the most gracious invitation in history and eternity.

This is the invitation into the worship-led life: to be forgiven of our fallen foray into the me-driven world; to receive the rescue for sinners and the ransom from heaven—indeed, to be reconciled to God; to be restored to the preciousness of sons and daughters of a good, good Father who can sing, "I am loved by you. It's who I am." The invitation is to be returned to our destiny as worshipers who rebuild the ruins of lost towns and corrupted cities, reclaiming wayward generations as holy unto the Lord. This invitation, born of the longing love of the Father, would cost Him His only Son:

But God demonstrates his own love for us in this: While we were still sinners, Christ died for us. Romans 5:8

Look how the great Prophet Isaiah spoke of this:

But he was pierced for our transgressions, he was crushed for our iniquities; the punishment that brought us peace was on him, and by his wounds we are healed. We all, like sheep, have gone astray, each of us has turned to our own way; and the LORD has laid on him the iniquity of us all. Isaiah 53:5–6

Sing with me . . .

Jesus Messiah, name above all names
Blessed redeemer, Emmanuel
The rescue for sinners, the ransom from Heaven
Jesus Messiah, Lord of all

For the wages of sin is death, but the gift of God is eternal life in Christ Jesus our Lord. Romans 6:23

This is the great worship leader—Jesus Messiah— who was prophesied by the prophets, who came from Heaven, who was born of a virgin, who was like Adam in every way except for sin, indeed who conquered sin and destroyed death.

Who, being in very nature God, did not consider equality with God something to be used to his own advantage; rather, he made himself nothing by taking the very nature of a servant, being made in human likeness. And being found in appearance as a man,

*he humbled himself by becoming obedient to death—
even death on a cross!* Philippians 2:6–8

His name is Jesus.

He paid a debt He did not owe because we owed a debt we could not pay. This was the day that love ran red down the altar of the cross, as the whole earth trembled and the veil was torn.

Therefore God exalted him to the highest place and gave him the name that is above every name, that at the name of Jesus every knee should bow, in heaven and on earth and under the earth, and every tongue acknowledge that Jesus Christ is Lord, to the glory of God the Father. Philippians 2:9–11

He did not come to make a name for Himself, for He would be given the name that is above every name. Sing with me . . .

Name above all names
Worthy of our praise
My heart will sing
How great is our God

He did not come to make Himself something. He was already everything. Instead, He made Himself nothing. He came to invite us to believe and be baptized in His name. This is the worship-led life, and He is the worship leader. This is the only way out of the me-driven world.

Here's the most beautiful part: the person who lives a worship-led life—by virtue of the One they are following—leads others out of the me-driven world and into a worship-led life. Jesus leads the journey from the brokenness of sin to the love of sons and daughters and onward to the blessedness of all of life by becoming the broken and poured-out love for the whole world.

Sing with me . . .

Nobody loves me like You love me, Jesus
I stand in awe of Your amazing ways
I worship You as long as I am breathing
God, You are faithful and true
Nobody loves me like You

So here we are. Standing at the brokenness of His altar together, where we receive His invitation: to step out of the me-driven world and into the worship-led life. The invitation is to exchange our sinfulness for His righteousness; our brokenness for His wholeness; our emptiness for His fullness; our ashes for His beauty; our mourning for His joy; our selfishness for His selflessness; our alias for His name.

He is calling out to you and to me:
Where are you?

Let's turn the question around and ask it of Jesus. Hear Him answer:

Here I am! I stand at the door and knock. If anyone hears my voice and opens the door, I will come in and eat with that person, and they with me.
Revelation 3:20

When we open the door to Jesus, we find ourselves at a table of fellowship around which we will feast forever.

PART I

UPWARD

Holy Forever

*Day and night they never stop
saying: "'Holy, holy, holy is the Lord
God Almighty,' who was, and is,
and is to come."* **Revelation 4:8**

Holy! Holy! Holy!
Growing up, it was always the first song in our hymnal.

Holy! Holy! Holy!
Lord God Almighty!

And looking back on those early days at that small church in East Texas, it seems like we sang it every single Sunday.

Early in the morning, our song shall rise to Thee.

For my brothers and me, after a Saturday full of sports, it did feel pretty early in the morning. Even so, this song shaped us. It formed our imaginations and filled our spirits with true worship. This was not a song about us or anything we had done or were doing or would ever do. It was not a song about what God had done or could do or would do for us, good as those kinds of songs are. Though I didn't pay much attention to song lyrics in those early days, I somehow knew this one was different. Because it was the first song in the book, I considered it my own first song.

In that little church so long ago, we knew that when we were singing this song, we weren't thinking about ourselves at all. In fact, it felt like we weren't even in the building anymore. As the Holy Spirit tuned our voices, weaving them together in melody and harmony, He transported us through the skies, into the heavens and before the very throne of Almighty God.

Holy! Holy! Holy!
Merciful and Mighty
God in Three Persons
Blessed Trinity

As we sang, we became lost to ourselves, our problems, our concerns, our brokenness, and even our blessings. And as we became lost to ourselves, we became found in God, on the inside of the holy community of the Blessed Trinity: Father, Son, and Holy Spirit. What a fellowship! What a joy divine! But that's another song, isn't it?

Holy! Holy! Holy!

Holy! It is the oldest song in the book because it's older than the book. It's the song of the angels and the archangels, of the elders and the living creatures. Holy! It's the song that transcends time—before the past and beyond the future. Holy! It's not the song of God's activity but of God's identity.

> *Day and night they never stop saying: "'Holy, holy, holy is the Lord God Almighty,' who was, and is, and is to come."* Revelation 4:8

This is where worship begins, not with what God has done but with who God is. Worship begins and ends with the sheer beauty, awe, and glory of God, becoming captured and enraptured by the greatness of God. Only one word can capture this, forever and ever: *Holy!*

Holy Forever!

Growing up, as I began to lead worship, people would ask what I planned to do for a living. I remember when I finally got the courage to say I hoped to become a full-time worship leader. Sometimes a well-meaning elder would say something like, "Son, don't become so heavenly minded that you are of no earthly good." While I nodded my head in respect, inwardly my heart grieved. Something in me knew that was wrong. I would cling to God's Word and to Scriptures like this one:

> *Since, then, you have been raised with Christ, set your hearts on things above, where Christ is, seated at the right hand of God. Set your minds on things above, not on earthly things. For you died, and your life is now hidden with Christ in God. When Christ, who is your life, appears, then you also will appear with him in glory.* Colossians 3:1–4

That seems to say the more heavenly minded you become, the more earthly good you will do. As we lift our hearts and set our minds on things above, we become caught up in the heavenly vision. Nothing is more needed on earth than the vision of heaven. And what is this vision? Thanks for asking.

> *After this I looked, and there before me was a great multitude that no one could count, from every nation, tribe, people and language, standing before the throne and before the Lamb. They were wearing white robes and were holding palm branches in their hands. And they cried out in a loud voice:*
>
> *"Salvation belongs to our God, who sits on the throne, and to the Lamb."* Revelation 7:9–10

This is the worship of heaven that now rises up all over the earth. What could be more worthy of our lives than to join this on-earth-as-it-is-in-heaven movement? This is the worship-led life. The vision keeps going:

> *All the angels were standing around the throne and around the elders and the four living creatures. They fell down on their faces before the throne and worshiped God, saying:*
>
> *"Amen! Praise and glory and wisdom and thanks and honor and power and strength be to our God for ever and ever. Amen!"* Revelation 7:11–12

Can you see the vision?

A thousand generations falling down in worship
To sing the song of ages to the Lamb
And all who've gone before us and all who will believe
Will sing the song of ages to the Lamb

Your name is the highest
Your name is the greatest
Your name stands above them all
All thrones and dominions
All powers and positions
Your name stands above them all

From my first song to my last, these songs of heaven are the shaping influence. In the days ahead we will dig a deep well into these eternal songs. We will remember and reflect, ponder and pray, journal and sing our way forward. As we walk together deeper into the presence of God, we will find ourselves becoming more of who we were made to be as His people. We will find the heavenly vision breaking forth into our lives on this earth as we grow to walk by faith and not by sight.

And the angels cry, Holy
All creation cries, Holy
You are lifted high, Holy
Holy forever!

THE BRIDGE

"Day and night they never stop saying: 'Holy, holy, holy is the Lord God Almighty,' who was, and is, and is to come."

These words ring out at the center of all that is real as they are spoken before the throne of God. Begin to speak them aloud today, becoming aware that you are joining worship already in progress in heaven.

I want you to read and revel in Revelation 4 and 5. Then turn to Revelation 7:9–12. Become intimately familiar with these songs of heaven. Set up a campsite right in the middle of them.

SING WITH ME

Queue up the song "Holy Forever" from our playlist (www .christomlin.com/singwithme) and sing along with me. Pay attention to your posture—posture matters because it expresses the worship of our very bodies before God. You might want to come out of that comfortable chair and get into a kneeling or standing position.

HOW GREAT?

How have you perhaps misunderstood the word "Holy" in the past? How are you thinking about it now? What would it mean to have a holy imagination as it comes to seeing the greatness of God?

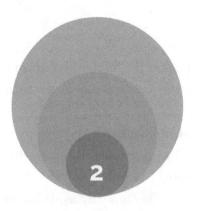

2

Holiness Unto the Lord
(We Fall Down)

've had the opportunity to be part of many music festivals over the years. One in particular stands out in my memory: Ichthus. I believe it was among the first Christian music festivals in the country—held in the tiny town of Wilmore, Kentucky, the year after the landmark Woodstock gathering.

While there for the festival in the early 2000s, I was given a tour of Asbury University. I'll never forget entering the chapel, because a sense of awe came over all of us. Between an expansive vaulted ceiling above and a tear-stained altar below stretched a thousand old-fashioned, ballpark-style wooden seats. The guides told us stories of history-making revivals in this very room, movements of the Holy Spirit that reached to the ends of the earth. All of this impressed me deeply, but what I remember most about that room were the four words etched into the oak beam at the peak of the front of the sanctuary—high and exalted above the room, serving as the focal point of the whole house:

Holiness Unto the Lord.

Though I had never seen this constellation of words anywhere before, I sensed they were already embedded deep in my heart. They instantly reminded me of one of the very first songs I ever wrote.

> We fall down. We lay our crowns at the feet of Jesus.
> The greatness of mercy and love at the feet of Jesus.
> And we cry HOLY, HOLY, HOLY is the Lamb.

Holiness Unto the Lord.

It's a curious phrase, isn't it? It comes from Zechariah 14:20 (KJV):

> *In that day shall there be upon the bells of the horses, HOLINESS UNTO THE LORD; and the pots in the LORD's house shall be like the bowls before the altar.*

That passage carries the notion that anything and everything touched by the Lord is set apart for Him and His service. From the bells on the horses to the common pots used for cooking—all of it is "holy unto the Lord."

For most of my life, I would have interpreted that phrase, *holiness unto the Lord*, as an admonition to behave. I thought of holiness primarily as good behavior, something we were supposed to do or not do, as the case may be.

Yet that phrase said something different to me this time. It spoke not so much of behavior or something we were supposed to do or not do. Holiness unto the Lord said something about identity, about the very nature of who I am and who you are. Once touched by the Lord, we are holy unto the Lord. We belong to Him. We are set apart for Him.

Now we are getting down to the very crux of the worship-led life: belonging to Jesus. Holiness means belonging to Jesus. Because He is holy, we are holy. It's why the Bible repeatedly says things like:

> *But just as he who called you is holy, so be holy in all*
> *you do: for it is written: "Be holy, because I am holy."*
> 1 Peter 1:15–16

We can't do holy unless we be holy. And we can't be holy apart from the very holiness of Jesus. We are who we are because of whose we are. Because Jesus is holy unto the Lord and Jesus is in us, we are holy unto the Lord.

Now, fast-forward with me twenty years.

It was winter 2023. My phone was blowing up with texts and calls. People were messaging me about a revival breaking out in Kentucky at—you guessed it—Asbury University. At the end of a regular chapel service, a small group of students stuck around to pray at the altar, and days later the chapel service was still ongoing. People were coming from far and wide by the thousands to experience this work of God. So why were they texting me? They wanted me to know that one of the songs they were singing on repeat was one of my oldest songs. Yes, you guessed it: "We Fall Down."

We fall down. We lay our crowns at the feet of Jesus.
The greatness of mercy and love at the feet of Jesus.
And we cry HOLY, HOLY, HOLY, is the Lamb.

I scanned social media and there it was: image after image captured the front of that chapel, and flying like a banner over it all were those words etched into the eve of the house:

Holiness Unto the Lord.

The holiness of God beckons us to what is perhaps the core calling of the worship-led life: consecration unto the Lord. You may remember how in the Old Testament, everything used in the temple, and everyone who ministered within, had to be consecrated as holy unto the Lord. Consecration is about purity, and yet it's not how we may tend to think. It is not a purity that comes from trying to cleanse or purify oneself. It is the purity that comes from ownership. To become holy unto the Lord only comes from belonging wholly to the Lord. It doesn't begin with us but with God. At the cross of Jesus, God says, "All of me for all of you." And at the cross of Jesus, we receive this gift and respond with our lives back to God, "All of me for all of you."

This is the deepest essence of the worship-led life.

THE BRIDGE

My friend J. D. Walt has written a simple prayer of consecration that I like a lot. Many are praying it every day with him. I commend it to you today and tomorrow and the next day:

Jesus, I belong to you.

I lift up my heart to you.

I set my mind on you.

I fix my eyes on you.

I offer my body as a living sacrifice to you.

Jesus, we belong to you.

Praying in the name of the Father, and the Son,
    and the Holy Spirit, Amen.

SING WITH ME

Let's go old-school today—all the way back to the beginning with one of my oldest songs and maybe the best of all. Sometimes the simplest of songs can carry the deepest of messages. Queue up "We Fall Down" on the playlist (www.christomlin.com/singwithme) and let it lead you into a place of deep consecration today.

HOW GREAT?

Have you ever encountered this curious phrase—"Holiness unto the Lord"—before? What kind of thoughts and feelings does it evoke in you? What would it mean for your life to be consecrated as "Holiness unto the Lord"?

Ministry to the Lord

A s I look back across my years as a worship leader, I notice something that I consider a distinctive part of God's calling and assignment on my life: many of the songs I have written or co-written are you might call "vertical" songs—almost exclusively about worshipping God for God's sake.

Broadly speaking, there are two kinds of ministry and two kinds of songs: ministry to the Lord and ministry to the people. So songs tend to go one way or the other: songs of pure adoration and songs of deliverance. We need both. (The truth is, none of our songs are even remotely worthy of God or of His house, but in His mercy and grace, He receives what we bring.)

One of the things I kept hearing about the outpouring of the Holy Spirit at Asbury University was how the worship took on the overall quality of ministering unto the Lord. People kept texting me that songs like "We Fall Down" and "How Great Is Our God" were on repeat. You remember how we talked about that phrase written at the top of the Asbury chapel:

Holiness Unto the Lord.

Those words cry out this notion of ministry to the Lord. While we need both kinds of ministry, to the Lord and to the House (or the people), and while one of these approaches may not necessarily be more important than the other, one of them does take priority in sequence. Ministry to the Lord must come first.

Remember the beginning of the prayer Jesus taught us, the one we call the Lord's Prayer? It is, "Hallowed be thy name." To pray this prayer and really enter into it is to minister unto the Lord. Let that come first. But don't just mouth the words and move on. Let these words lead you into the movement of hallowing Him.

Years ago, I came across a fascinating message from the late Watchman Nee, a highly celebrated and persecuted church planter and preacher in China in the twentieth century. He was talking about the difference between ministering to the Lord and ministering to people:

"The conditions basic to all ministry that can truly be called ministry to the Lord are drawing near to Him and standing before Him. But how hard we often find it to drag ourselves into His presence! We shrink from the solitude, and even when we do detach ourselves physically, our thoughts still keep wandering outside. Many of us can enjoy working among people, but how many of us can draw near to God in the Holy of Holies? Yet it is only as we draw near to Him that we can minister to Him.

"Unless we really know what it is to draw near to God, we cannot know what it is to serve Him. It is impossible to stand afar off and still minister to Him. We cannot serve Him from a distance. There is only one place where ministry to Him is possible and that is in the Holy Place. In the outer court you approach the people; in the Holy Place you approach the Lord. Today we always want to be moving on; we cannot stand still. There are so many things claiming our attention that we are perpetually on the go. We cannot stop for a moment. But a spiritual person knows how to stand still. He can stand before God till God makes His will known."

Jesus told an interesting and challenging story concerning this priority:

> "Suppose one of you has a servant plowing or looking after the sheep. Will he say to the servant when he comes in from the field, 'Come along now and sit down to eat'? Won't he rather say, 'Prepare my supper, get yourself ready and wait on me while I eat and drink; after that you may eat and drink'?" Luke 17:7–8

If we want to live a worship-led life, we must learn the priority of ministering to the Lord. This means carving out the time, regularly, to come before the Lord for no other reason than His worthiness of our worship. Yes, we must come before the Lord on behalf of the needs of other people and in ministry to them. Yes, we should come before the

Lord on behalf of our own needs for mercy and grace and deliverance. Yes, we can sing all the songs. But ministry to the Lord must take priority and precedence. Because we are living in such a me-centered culture, it is easy to forget the priority of ministering to the Lord.

So how do we minister to the Lord? I love how the book of Hebrews issues this calling to us:

> *Therefore, brothers and sisters, since we have confidence to enter the Most Holy Place by the blood of Jesus, by a new and living way opened for us through the curtain, that is, his body, and since we have a great priest over the house of God, let us draw near to God with a sincere heart and with the full assurance that faith brings, having our hearts sprinkled to cleanse us from a guilty conscience and having our bodies washed with pure water.* Hebrews 10:19–22

When was the last time you came into the presence of God purely for God's sake? This means you came asking for nothing for yourself or for anyone else—no prayer list, no intercession, no petition, no confession, not even gratitude for answered prayers or blessings. Ministry to the Lord means blessing the Lord simply for the sake of who He is, not for what He has done, is doing, or will do. It may feel awkward, but try lifting your hands. You might sing a song like "We Fall Down" or "How Great is Our God." (There are many more from across the ages to choose from.) Invite the Holy Spirit to give you a song, a song that is for you and not for anyone else. Then sing it to God alone. Just start. Fight through the distraction that will come. In time you will find the inner sanctuary of the most holy place, and you will discover how the rest of life flows from here. The unhindered, unbridled presence of God will become the center of gravity in your existence.

This, my friends, is the place from which the worship-led life springs.

THE BRIDGE

We are given an extraordinary vision in Revelation 5 of all the angelic host encircling the throne of God. They are ministering unto the Lord, with great volume, making this eternal declaration:

> *"Worthy is the Lamb, who was slain, to receive power and wealth and wisdom and strength and honor and glory and praise!"* Revelation 5:12

John continues to unfold the vision of eternal doxology:

> *Then I heard every creature in heaven and on earth and under the earth and on the sea, and all that is in them, saying: "To him who sits on the throne and to the Lamb be praise and honor and glory and power, for ever and ever!"* (v. 13)

SING WITH ME

Can we sing our title track today? "How Great Is Our God." Let that flow back into one we've already shared, "Holy Forever." They are on our setlist. As you sing, ask the Holy Spirit to consecrate your very imagination as holy unto the Lord—that you may sense yourself participating in the great song of heaven this day.

HOW GREAT?

Are you grasping this concept of "Ministry to the Lord"? Do you have a secret place where you are able to approach God in this way? Does this give new depth to the phrase, "Hallowed be Your name?" How might you take a next step in this kind of worship?

The Phos Hilaron

There's a story from the early days of the Church in Jerusalem. Around evening time, as the sun was setting, Christians would gather just outside of Jesus's empty tomb for worship. From the resurrection forward, tradition tells us they kept a flaming lamp burning inside the tomb at all times. As they gathered, an acolyte would enter the empty tomb with an unlit candle, light it from the lamp, and then come forth to process through the people, lighting lanterns along the way. This part of the service was called "the lighting of the lamps." As the light of Christ was processing through, the gathered worshippers would sing the "Phos Hilaron," one of the earliest recorded hymns of the church outside of the Bible. I love this English translation of that ancient hymn:

> Hail, gladdening Light, of His pure glory poured
> Who is the immortal Father, heavenly, blest,
> Holiest of Holies, Jesus Christ our Lord!

Now we are come to the sun's hour of rest;
The lights of evening round us shine;
We hymn the Father, Son, and Holy Spirit divine!
Worthiest art Thou at all times to be sung
With undefiled tongue,
Son of our God, Giver of life, alone:
Therefore in all the world Thy glories, Lord,
     thine own.

Many years ago I wrote a song inspired by the "Phos Hilaron" and put it to melody. I called it "Joyous Light." I definitely like the ancient song title better. *Phos* means light. The Latin word *Hilaron* means exuberantly glad. Think hilarious. The hilarious light of Jesus. It laughs in the face of sin and death. John put it this way:

In him was life, and that life was the light of all mankind. The light shines in the darkness, and the darkness has not overcome it. John 1:4–5

Phos Hilaron: The light laughs at the darkness.

I tell you what I most love about this hymn: it's all about God. There is no cry for deliverance or blessing or provision. It is pure God. To be clear, it's not wrong to pray and sing about deliverance, blessing, provision, and help. The problem comes when we starting with ourselves and our own needs. We never really quite get to God alone. Here's what I have discovered to be true: When we start with worshipping God for God's own sake—what I call *pure God*—we find ourselves strangely delivered from worry and anxiety and fear. Our prayers for deliverance are answered without even being raised, so fixed is our worship on Him. I would give anything to write a song with the songwriter who penned words like these:

> Hail, gladdening Light, of His pure glory poured
> Who is the immortal Father, heavenly, blest,
> Holiest of Holies, Jesus Christ our Lord!

Notice how the song causes us to fix our full and complete attention on God alone: Father, Son, and Holy Spirit. The worship-led life is simultaneously about becoming totally focused on God and growing completely self-forgetful. In fact, the only way to become self-forgetful is to become fixed on God. Ironically, the more you try to forget yourself, the more you focus on yourself. When self is the reference point, there is no escape. When Jesus is the reference point, we live in the orbit of the greatness of God with no thought for ourselves. As our false self fades away, our true life emerges, and it is a life of true worship. The worship-led life is about becoming "lost in wonder love and praise," as another great hymn writer penned it.

Jesus said it like this:

> *"If anyone would come after me, let him deny himself and take up his cross daily and follow me."*
> Luke 9:23 ESV

There is only one way to deny yourself and take up your cross: by following Jesus. We don't forget ourselves by trying to forgive ourselves, else He wouldn't have had to come. We forget ourselves by following Jesus, by keeping our eyes fixed on Him who is "Holiest of Holies, Jesus Christ our Lord!"

From the earliest days of the Church, the people of God have found innovative and interesting ways to keep their eyes fixed on Jesus. One way is called the Daily Office—seven times of prayer each day corresponding with biblical points of reference and especially the life, death, and resurrection of Jesus:

- Lauds (praise) corresponds with sunrise and the resurrection of Jesus.
- Terce (third hour, 9 a.m.) corresponds with Jesus being nailed to the cross.
- Sext (sixth hour, noon) corresponds with Jesus praying from the cross.
- None (ninth hour, 3 p.m.) corresponds with Jesus's death on the cross.
- Vespers (evening) corresponds with Jesus laid in the tomb.
- Compline (retiring for sleep) marks the end of the day.
- Vigils (middle of the night) corresponds with Paul and Silas praying in prison.

Do you know who invented clocks with ringing bells? The Church. They did this so that all within hearing of the bells could be called to remember Jesus and to worship and pray throughout the day. Are you getting the picture? We stand on the shoulders of giants who lived worship-led lives. While I don't practice the Daily Office, I want to live inspired by it. This encourages me to flip my script, remembering that God does not revolve around me but I revolve around Him. My life of worship is about revolving my story around God's glory.

Now, where were we? Vespers! We are gathered with the early Christians in Jerusalem outside the empty tomb. The sun is setting. We are singing.

> Now we are come to the sun's hour of rest;
> The lights of evening round us shine;
> We hymn the Father, Son, and Holy Spirit divine!

Darkness is falling. This is the hour when Jesus was taken down from the cross and laid in the borrowed tomb. And those lanterns, lit by the flame from the now-empty tomb, are blazing bright. Hail gladdening light. The Son, dead at sundown and sealed in the tomb, is now risen in the darkness, dealing defeat to the night.

The last time I checked, the sun rises in the eastern sky, makes its pilgrimage across the vault of the sky, and sets on the western horizon every single day. Yes, this is an every single day opportunity. Shall we?

> We hymn the Father.
> We hymn the Son.
> We hymn the Spirit.
> Holy Divine.
> No-one more worthy of songs to be sung
> To the giver of Life
> All Glory is Thine.

THE BRIDGE

I will forever remember hearing the voices of my friends Shane & Shane at the OneDay03 gathering in Sherman, Texas, in 2003. As we entered the Vespers hour and the sun was setting, they began to lead a one-line song from Psalm 113:

> *From the rising of the sun to the place where it sets, the name of the LORD is to be praised.* Psalm 113:3

After repeating it a few times, they began to sing out, "Praise Ye the Lord" over and over again. It was so simple and so profound. I had never heard it sung like that before or since, but it captures the worship-led life, doesn't it? What if you hide this single verse in your deep memory—repeating it upon rising and then upon retiring each day? Have you ever noticed how we can go through entire days without ever seeing a sunrise or a sunset or even noticing the sun, for that matter? Meanwhile, it is sustaining our lives the entire time. How much more is this the case with our God? How might we reorient our awareness and attention to worship Jesus?

SING WITH ME

I'm digging deep into the archives to pull out "Joyous Light" for us to sing today. You will find it in the playlist (www.christomlin.com/singwithme). Maybe find a place to watch the sunset today, and let's sing it together in praise of our great God.

HOW GREAT?

When is the last time you found yourself so in the presence of God that you seemed to "lose" yourself in His greatness? What might prayer and worship through the hours of the day look like for you? How might the ancient practice of the Daily Office inspire and help you?

The Earth Is Filled With His Glory

Have you ever thought about the relationship between nature and the worship-led life? I love nature. I enjoy few things more than getting out in the beauty of God's creation. I love the beauty of a waterfall, or the ocean or a forest . . . because they are filled with the greatness of God.

Our soul knows a deep connection with creation because it continually points to God's glory. Nature has a way of resizing us, a gentle way of reminding us that we are not as great as we think we are. However, creation is not the Creator. Let's not get that confused.

It always stuns me when people say they don't like to go to church because they can worship God better when they are out in nature. This isn't a good excuse, unfortunately. Down through the centuries, apart from the church, people have pretty much worshipped nature. It is a short step from there to making nature your God. Instead, the more I go out into the beauty of nature, the more I want to worship God *with* His Church.

Here's what I've learned about the worship of God and the place of creation: God created a very good world, but as good as creation is, creation is not God. In fact, creation does not reveal God. Only God can reveal Himself. Paul put it well in his letter to the Romans:

> *For since the creation of the world God's invisible qualities—his eternal power and divine nature—have been clearly seen, being understood from what has been made, so that people are without excuse.* Romans 1:20

Creation points to God, but it does not reveal Him. Creation is filled with the glory of God, but even the glory of God is not God. God is not *in* His creation. Rather, God is completely *other than* His creation. In fact, in Genesis 1, as we read the story of creation, God never says creation is holy. The first thing God deems holy is time itself—the seventh day, a holy day set apart to rest and to respond in worship to the God of all creation. We do not "find" God in nature. We find God's glory in nature, which is meant to point us to God. If we miss this seemingly small distinction, we will wind up in the place Paul described later in chapter 1 of Romans:

> *They exchanged the truth about God for a lie, and worshiped and served created things rather than the Creator—who is forever praised. Amen.* Romans 1:25

Translation: Enjoy nature. Worship God.

The worship-led life begins, middles, and ends in the exalted, holy, otherness of God and God alone. Get this clear in your mind: Enjoy nature. Worship God. Let's take it a step further.

In Isaiah 6, the prophet shared with us his vision of worship. In his vision he saw the Lord, high and exalted, and the train of His robe filled the temple. Isaiah said there were angelic beings called seraphim flying above God. We don't know how many of them there were, but each had six wings. With two wings they covered their faces. With two wings they covered their feet. And with the other two wings they were flying. And the Scripture says they were calling out to each other these words:

> *"Holy, holy, holy is the Lord Almighty; the whole earth is full of his glory."* Isaiah 6:3

I once put those exact words to song so the Church could sing it:

> We stand and lift up our hands
> For the joy of the Lord is our strength
> We bow down and worship Him now
> How great, how awesome is He.
> And together we sing
> Holy is the Lord, God Almighty
> The earth is filled with His glory

While many people loved the song, I don't think it even came close to doing justice to Isaiah's vision. I mean, this is what the Bible says happened in response to the crying out of the seraphim:

*At the sound of their voices the doorposts and thresh-
olds shook and the temple was filled with smoke.*
Isaiah 6:4

In other words, this was not a sweet new song playing
on your local K-LOVE affiliate.

This verse reminds me of being on the road with Francis Chan one time when he started talking about angelic
beings. We were leading together at a summer camp, and
I was having trouble connecting with the young people on
one particular night. As I was leading, most were apathetic
at best and some quite disrespectful of the moment.

Francis abruptly took the stage and began describing
these angelic beings. He said, "Can you imagine if one of
these creatures showed up on this stage right now . . . a
massive creature with six wings, full of eyes—a being we
have never ever conceived? We would all be running out
of the building; there would be lots of screams, people
getting under their chairs. Pandemonium! And yet the
Bible tells us these creatures hide their face in the presence of the holiness of God. . . . How can we be so apathetic in our worship? We need a new vision of who we
worship tonight!"

Let me tell you, the room changed. Everyone got
the point.

Anyway, as we were saying . . .

*At the sound of their voices the doorposts and thresholds
shook and the temple was filled with smoke.*

I want us to notice what the seraphim were saying and
what they were not saying:

"Holy, holy, holy is the Lord Almighty;
the whole earth is full of his glory."

God is not in the same category as the earth. God is not even remotely part of His creation. As I've said, God is completely other than His creation. This is part of what it means when we say God is holy. It means God is completely *other*. Now that we have that clear, yes, the whole earth is full of His glory.

Holy, holy, holy is the Lord Almighty =
    Worship God!
The whole earth is full of His glory = Enjoy nature!

And one more thing: think again before skipping church to go fishing (just kidding, sort of . . .).

THE BRIDGE

I particularly love the bridge of the song "Holy Is the Lord." It goes like this:

It's rising up all around.
It's the anthem of the Lord's renown.

The anthem, of course, is Isaiah 6:3.

"Holy, holy, holy is the LORD Almighty; the whole earth is full of his glory."

I want this verse to become deeply embedded in our minds and hearts in such a way that it changes the way we see the earth. We are praying for the supernatural ability to perceive the glory of God in the natural world. I want us to begin declaring this verse all through the day, particularly as we are outside and moving about. Journal about how this impacts you.

SING WITH ME

Dial up the song "Holy Is the Lord" on our playlist (www .christomlin.com/singwithme) and sing it with me. Sing particularly loud on the chorus and even louder on the bridge.

HOW GREAT?

How does creation lift your soul to fathom the greatness and glory of God? How might you grow in your awareness of the whole of creation worshipping God—mountains bowing down, seas roaring, trees of the field clapping their hands? What might it look like for you to join creation's song of praise?

Everywhere I Go I See You

Have you ever realized how the whole earth is always pointing to God? One of my heroes is the late Rich Mullins. Rich was a songwriter and worship leader before being a songwriter and worship leader was a thing. It brings to mind that old Barbara Mandrell country song, "I was country when country wasn't cool." Well, Rich Mullins was about worship when worship wasn't cool. He was writing songs like "Our God Is an Awesome God" before the radio would even play worship songs. That's another story.

Rich lived a worship-led life. Was he rough around the edges? Yes. Was he offensive to the religious status quo? Yes. Did he have his accountant pay him the average salary of a blue-collar worker in America year after year and give the rest away? Yes! If there were any artist I wish I could have known, it was him. Rich had this song called "I See You." It was one of those call-and-response songs we love so much. He would sing a line, and the people would echo it.

The song told of being led by a cloud by day and a pillar of fire by night. He sang of rivers and sunrises, of eagles and night skies. Through the whole song, woven throughout all the imagery of creation, he repeated this refrain:

And everywhere I go I see you.

Isn't that what Scripture is saying over and over again?

The heavens declare the glory of God; the skies proclaim the work of his hands. Day after day they pour forth speech; night after night they reveal knowledge. Psalm 19:1–2

And everywhere I go I see you.

In the heavens God has pitched a tent for the sun. It is like a bridegroom coming out of his chamber, like a champion rejoicing to run his course. It rises at one end of the heavens and makes its circuit to the other; nothing is deprived of its warmth. Psalm 19:4–6

And everywhere I go I see you.

From ancient times and all the way to the present day, fallen and broken human beings have worshipped everything under the sun (and including the sun). God's Word reveals that God not only created the sun, but He also pitched a tent for it and called it the sky. Further, the sun puts on a daily show, racing across the sky and declaring the glory of God as it goes.

And everywhere I go I see you.

People will worship the stars and even consult constellations for daily guidance. Meanwhile, the God who made them all cries out in silent speech through creation. Do not worship the sun and stars. Bow down before the One who made them. One of the big keys to the worship-led life is allowing what we see with our eyes to lift our souls to what can only be seen by the eyes of our hearts. Learning to see what is unseen through what is visible.

And everywhere I go I see you.

Treat all of creation and nature not as beautiful imagery you look at but as iconic reality you see through. Look through them as dynamic portals, opening up a line of sight to the unseen One to whom they point.

And everywhere I go I see you.

Several years back, the band and I were invited to Kauai to host a worship night for the island. (Those are the requests you don't have to pray much about.) Nicknamed "the Garden Island," Kauai is crazy beautiful, with gorgeous mountains bending to the bluest of blue ocean, separated by what seems like perfectly curated sand. The refrain of Rich's song reverberated like my heartbeat the whole time: "And everywhere I go I see you."

On Kauai, we were given the opportunity to take a helicopter tour. I wasn't ready. For one, I don't particularly like flying. But more than that, I wasn't ready for what I was about to see and feel.

The pilot gave us headphones and piped in the John Williams soundtrack of *Jurassic Park* as he flew us literally through waterfalls and into canyons. At one point, he dropped us in the cone of a dormant volcano whose rim was dressed with at least fifty waterfalls. Then the pilot said, "I'm saving the best for last."

I couldn't imagine it getting any more beautiful. We began to fly away from the island until all we could see from the windshield of that chopper was the vast Pacific Ocean—a sea of blue. Then the pilot came over our headphones and said, "What you are about to see can only be seen from a helicopter or a boat." He slowly began to spin the helicopter in a 180, and we were staring right back at the island from a distance. I literally lost my breath. The pilot said, "You are looking at the Cathedrals." This mountain range juts out of the far end of Kauai—massive green spires reaching into the heavens. The English language truly fails when trying to describe it.

Suddenly, my eyes began to water. I wasn't ready for that—especially crammed into a helicopter with a bunch of dudes! My physical body could not handle the beauty. It was like my heart knew in some way that it was made for Eden. I was overwhelmed, and tears began to flow. Even now as I write this, I still feel the glory of those mountains. I also can't help but wonder how many more "cathedrals" exist in this vast universe that God has made.

And everywhere I go I see you.

THE BRIDGE

All of this brings the eighth Psalm to mind.

When I consider your heavens, the work of your fingers, the moon and the stars, which you have set in place, what is mankind that you are mindful of them, human beings that you care for them? You have made

*them a little lower than the angels and crowned them
with glory and honor.* Psalm 8:3–5

After creating all the world, God created us. I was part
of an incredible song years ago called "Indescribable." Back
when we were singing it a lot, I loved to bridge back and
forth between these lines:

"You placed the stars in the sky and you know
them by name. You are amazing, God."
"You see the depths of my heart and you love me
the same. You are amazing, God."

I would like us to walk around in Psalm 8 today and
ponder these indescribable, uncontainable realities of a
worship-led life.

SING WITH ME

Pull up the Rich Mullins song referenced today, "I See You."
It's in our playlist (www.christomlin.com/singwithme). Pair
that with "Indescribable." These two songs will set the stage
for the glorious day ahead.

HOW GREAT?

Can you remember an occasion or experience where you
were undone by the glory of God in His creation? How
aware are you of the glory God has invested in the creation
of you? Have you awakened to the sheer glory of who you
are as an image-bearer of the living God?

The Songs That Never Grow Old

Over the years I have led worship in a lot of large venues. Some favorite moments that come to mind are the Hollywood Bowl in LA, Madison Square Garden in New York City, and a field of forty thousand or so people gathered somewhere outside Kampala, Uganda. That night in Uganda was one of the longest nights of playing music for me ever, and I loved every second. You see, the majority of people had traveled for hours, even days, to be there and no way were they going to be satisfied with a normal "American ninety-minute set" of songs. I think we played every song we knew at least twice that night.

I also recall another instance of when people wouldn't leave during a two-night show at Red Rocks Amphitheatre outside Denver. First, if you ever get a chance to see and hear music at Red Rocks, take it. It's beyond special. God created the most beautiful natural setting you can imagine. But what makes me remember these nights was the weather. It poured down rain for an entire two-hour set for *both* nights, and it was about forty-two degrees outside, but almost everyone stayed for the whole show. My fingers could barely move across the guitar strings, they were so cold. But the people! Wow. . . . As I looked out on a sea of rain ponchos, there was a new meaning to the lyrics "like a flood His mercy rains unending love, amazing grace." I love singing to God in places like these.

I have sat in small rooms off to the side of these massive places with worship leaders. I love to spend time with worship leaders. They "get" the worship-led life more than most. I especially love to spend time with those leaders who know that worship is more than just singing. That's the thing about a worship-led life, isn't it? Songs are just the soundtrack. Our lives count the most. How are our everyday lives leading the worship of God in our everyday world?

Back to those little meetings in the small rooms with worship leaders. They always ask tons of great questions, many of which I can't begin to answer. They want to know how to write better songs, how to fade into the background while at the center of the stage, how to know when to speak and when not to speak, how to be both planned and spontaneous, and I could go on. I admit that some of their questions bother me, especially this one: "How do you keep singing the same songs night after night after night? Don't you ever get tired of these songs?" I always want to ask them in return (though I never do), "Do you ever get tired of the same God week after week after week?"

Instead, I say to them and to you and to anyone and everyone: the songs themselves are not what's most important; it's the meaning behind them; it's who the songs are for. I'll bet I have been to ten thousand sporting events over the course of my life, and at every single one of those events we sing the same song. We always sing the national anthem, "The Star-Spangled Banner." And you know what? I never get tired of singing that song. From what I see around me, no one else does either. Why is that? Because of what the song is about. "The Star-Spangled Banner" lifts our hearts and minds to the greatness of a nation, to the cost of freedom, to the trauma and the drama of battle, and to the nobility of bravery it inspires.

If we never tire of singing about a great nation, how could we ever tire of singing glorious songs about our great God—even the same songs over and over? My old friend Matt Redman said it best in his classic song "The Heart of Worship":

> "I'll bring you more than a song, for a song in itself
> is not what you have required."

Sometimes people get focused on the kind of experience a particular song gives them in worship. They come away from a gathering saying things like, "The worship was amazing" or, "That song was really something." Or they mutter, "They are really overplaying this song" or, "I am getting burned out on that one." To me, this is a sign we have missed the point.

People get tired of songs because they no longer have the same kind of experience in worship with the song they once did. We want to walk away from a gathering of God's people not talking about the power of the songs or the worship or our experience of it all but about the greatness of God. When is the last time you walked out of a great movie and all you wanted to talk about was the soundtrack? No! You wanted to rave about the movie. Songs are the soundtrack. Worship is the life. And as we grow in the worship-led life, the songs never get old.

THE BRIDGE

With ten words, the writer of the ancient book we call Hebrews penned an anchor for the ages—one of those banners ever flying over the worship-led life:

> *Jesus Christ is the same yesterday and today and forever.* Hebrews 13:8

That phrase is one of the most simple, profound, and powerful creeds in all of the Bible. However, unless we get it out of the Bible and into the world, it will stay locked inside. We must loose the words of Scripture from their bookish bindings and unleash them in our lives. This begins by speaking them aloud so our ears can hear them. Remember, faith comes by hearing. As we hear the words over and over, the Spirit etches them on our hearts and grooves them like a vinyl record on our souls. Will you speak that Hebrews passage aloud right now, as an affirmation of your faith? Say it a few times. Get a dry-erase marker and write it on your bathroom mirror. Copy it on a slip of paper and tape it to the dashboard of your car.

SING WITH ME

I've got two songs for us today on the playlist (www .christomlin.com/singwithme)—one of my oldest songs and one of my newest. Let's start with the new one. It is called "Always," and I think you will quickly see why I have chosen it. The old one is called "Forever." I have led it thousands of times by now and it never gets old. Let's get lost in God today as we sing these songs to Him. And for good measure, let's also sing Matt Redman's "10,000 Reasons."

HOW GREAT?

Have you ever found yourself being more focused on the song than on who the song is leading us to worship? How can we keep songs and even our own individual experience in perspective? How might we find our way back to the heart of worship?

PART II

INWARD

Jesus Is the Worship Leader

One of the most obvious and yet most overlooked things about the worship-led life is this: a person cannot live a worship-led life unless they are following a worship leader. And I'm not talking about the person leading songs from the stage. The truth is, we are all following worship leaders of one sort or another. These days we call them "influencers." Most are calling us deeper into the me-driven world. They want to influence us to live like they live and do what they do and buy their products and emulate their lifestyles. It's really kind of sick, but when you think about it, this is exactly what they are doing. Before we know it, we have flicked our phone screen fifty times and gone through every picture and every reel and clicked through many of their links to delve deeper and deeper into their lives.

We actively, yet often unknowingly, emulate the people we follow. The real question is: Who are we following? The point of this whole book is to call you to the only worship leader worthy of following: Jesus. Let me say it clearly:

The worship leader is Jesus.

By following Jesus we enter the worship-led life. The Bible is always talking about things like "opening the eyes of my heart" and "fixing our eyes on Jesus" and "listening for the still, small whisper of God." But how do we do this? How do we know this is God and not just our own interests and agendas we are claiming as God's will—projecting our own thoughts onto the mind of God? This is where the Word of God, the Bible, comes into play. Because we have to train ourselves to be still and listen for the voice of God through the Holy Spirit for guidance.

The Bible is not a book telling us what to believe and how to behave. The Bible is showing us how to behold and who to become. That's what the worship-led life is all about: learning to behold Jesus and, in beholding Him, becoming like Him. We don't become like Him by trying harder and harder to behave like Him. No, we become like Him as we behold Him. The Holy Spirit transforms our lives by filling us with His life. The Bible exhorts us to have the same mind in us that was in Jesus.

The worship-led life invites us to become completely immersed and even obsessed with the actual life of the worship leader we are following. Think of it like this: The world's greatest artists all began their work by copying the work of the great artists who went before them. They studied their patterns, their color compositions, their brushstrokes, their vision and ways of seeing. They wanted to get inside an artist's mind. They did this by studying their work and then copying it. They worked by imitation.

Through this process, something of the artist was mysteriously imparted to them. Imitation became impartation, which led to improvisation. Van Gogh didn't just pull his famous painting of The Sower out of the sky of his imagination. No, he started following the art of Jean-Francois Millet, whose painting of a peasant sowing seed captured Van Gogh's imagination. He began by making direct copies, and one day he painted his own imaginative version, anchored in the work of Millet and yet completely new.

I'll be honest. For too long in my own life, I had a truncated view of the Gospels. I saw them as the crucifixion and resurrection of Jesus. Certainly, this is their point, but somewhere along the way I began to see them as God painting with words. And isn't that what John says: "The Word became flesh and made his dwelling among us" (John 1:14). I began to see the cross as much deeper than six hours on Good Friday. I started to see it as His whole life—painted in the words of every scene. One day I was reading Romans and came across this verse:

> For if, while we were God's enemies, we were reconciled to him through the death of his Son, how much more, having been reconciled, shall we be saved through his life! Romans 5:10

Insert mind-blown emoji here. If we are reconciled by His death, how much more will we be saved through His life. Wow! I want to become a student of Jesus's life, His every move, His every encounter, His every word. Jesus is the worship leader, and He is the only worship leader we actually worship. Now, when I survey the wondrous cross, I see His whole life unfold. The cross rises up from the wedding in Cana of Galilee to the miraculous mystery of the multiplied fishes and loaves to the healing of a man born blind to a woman who pours out a year's wages on His feet in the form of an alabaster jar of perfume.

Every step of the way, Jesus is worshipping His Father, and at the same time He is leading us to worship Him. This is why He is the only one worthy to break the seal and open the scroll and become the subject, verb, and object of endless ages of worship Himself.

THE BRIDGE

Becoming like Jesus comes not from striving harder to behave like Him but from learning to behold Him. The following verse is a worship-led life verse. I commend it to you as the curriculum of your life:

> *And we all, with unveiled face, beholding the glory of the Lord, are being transformed into the same image from one degree of glory to another. For this comes from the Lord who is the Spirit.* 2 Corinthians 3:18 ESV

I want us to start approaching the Gospels (Matthew, Mark, Luke, and John) differently. Rather than reading them for information, how about we behold Jesus in them for transformation? It is a different posture. It is the posture of worship. Yes, beholding is the posture of worship.

SING WITH ME

I have written a lot of songs about Jesus over the years, and we will sing several of them here. Today, let's sing "Jesus Messiah." I like how the song points to a couple of powerful Gospel stories. As we sing, let's invite the Holy Spirit to transform our singing into beholding. Pull it up in the playlist (www.christomlin.com/singwithme) and give it a go. And how about we add to this Brooke Ligertwood's "What a Beautiful Name" today?

HOW GREAT?

How much does the actual life of Jesus factor into your worship? Have you awakened to Jesus as the great worship leader? Have you found ways to "behold" Jesus through reading the accounts of His glorious life?

9

White Flag

A worship-led life is a life of surrender.

I love the old hymn "I Surrender All." In fact, I love a lot of old hymns. Something about the old songs—they never get old. Rather, they get even better with age. "I Surrender All" is one of the standards of the worship-led life. Let's take a minute and rehearse those brilliant lyrics from Judson W. Van De Venter:

> All to Jesus I surrender,
> All to Him I freely give;
> I will ever love and trust Him,
> In His presence daily live.
>
> All to Jesus I surrender,
> Make me, Savior, wholly Thine;
> Let me feel Thy Holy Spirit,
> Truly know that Thou art mine.

All to Jesus I surrender,
Lord, I give myself to Thee;
Fill me with Thy love and power,
Let Thy blessing fall on me.

I surrender all, I surrender all;
All to Thee, my blessed Savior,
I surrender all.

I have many memories of this song sung around the altars of my growing-up years. Inspired by it, I wrote a new song about surrender some years ago called "White Flag." In the world's eyes, surrender is the ultimate sign of weakness. In the eyes of God, it is the ultimate sign of worship, because a worship-led life is a life of surrender.

Something deep in us all resists surrender. For centuries the universal sign of surrender in battle has involved waving a white flag—admitting defeat. Yet consider the amazing reality of the cross of Jesus: that cross stands as both the sign of surrender and the sign of salvation. The cross is the sign of utter defeat *and* ultimate victory. In fact, at the cross, defeat transformed into victory and death led to resurrection. That is what I am trying to say through my song "White Flag":

We raise our white flag
We surrender all to You, all for you
We raise our white flag: the war is over
Love has come, your love has won

It is one thing to sing about surrender and quite another to actually do it. There is a secret pathway to surrender.

We see it revealed in the most difficult moment of Jesus's life, just after the Last Supper on the last night. Jesus and His disciples found themselves in a familiar place facing an unfathomable moment. He asked Peter, James, and John to come away with Him and keep watch over Him as He withdrew to draw near to God. I love how the Bible tells us He withdrew about a stone's throw from the three. This reminds me that in the hardest situations we may face, the path of surrender is always near to us—no more than a stone's throw away. Let's cut to the highlight reel of Scripture to see the pathway to surrender unfold:

> *"Father, if you are willing, take this cup from me; yet not my will, but yours be done." An angel from heaven appeared to him and strengthened him. And being in anguish, he prayed more earnestly, and his sweat was like drops of blood falling to the ground."*
> Luke 22:42–44

Jesus articulated His desire. Then He abandoned Himself to God. With a mere seven words, He shows us the secret of surrender: "Not my will, but yours be done."

Our default prayer is just the opposite: "Not your will, but mine be done." We would never be so bold as to speak it to God; nevertheless, we shout it with our lives. We find this epitaph over the grave of Adam: *Not your will, but mine be done.* Note the stark difference: Adam's grave is filled with the bones of billions; Jesus's grave is empty.

So why is the worship-led life so hard? For starters, perhaps because we think it should be easy. Though we sing all day long about surrender, surrender can't be reduced to a song. Surrender is not a feeling (passion-filled as the act may be). We might picture ourselves as Sir William Wallace, willingly and passionately running straight into the face of death, come what may. But Jesus did not channel His inner Sir William Wallace. No, He presented His true self in the presence of His Abba Father. He clearly expressed His will in the garden of Gethsemane—asking that the cup of suffering pass him by. He knew that surrender involves suffering, and He did not want to suffer the torture He knew was on its way to Him.

The worship-led life requires that we become brazenly real and brutally honest about our own will. Then and only then can we make the turn to the transformational grace of surrender and the seven words that slay Satan: *not my will, but yours be done.* When we fail to be honest about our own will, coming clean about our own ambition and interest, we slide into the slipstream of self-deception. From there we unwittingly make the fateful leap into the assumption of our will and God's will as one and the same.

There is another equally dangerous self-deception at work here: none of us sees God as He truly is. Because of our own brokenness and the broken relationships in our past, notably in our families of origin, we often live with the unconscious assumption that if we want or will something good for ourselves, it must not be God's will. We assume God does not want what we want. Again, the antidote is surrender and trust that the will of God is the best life possible.

The seven words of surrender—not my will, but yours be done—unfold a long path of sublimating our self-interest to the greatest good of the will of God. Every time we say them in the secret place before God, we are raising our white flag. Indeed, this is the white flag of a surrendered life. I love the way the song reaches its peak and breaks out into a jubilant celebration:

> We lift the cross, lift it high, lift it high!
> We lift the cross, lift it high, lift it high!
> We lift the cross, lift it high, lift it high!
> We lift the cross, lift it high, lift it high!

THE BRIDGE

In Luke 9 Jesus makes a stunning speech about surrender. He says some of the hardest, most truthful things imaginable. Here's an example:

> "*Whoever wants to be my disciple must deny themselves and take up their cross daily and follow me.* Luke 9:23

Then He doubles down with this:

> *For whoever wants to save their life will lose it, but whoever loses their life for me will save it.* Luke 9:24

And if that weren't clear enough, Jesus takes it a step further:

> *What good is it for someone to gain the whole world, and yet lose or forfeit their very self?* Luke 9:25

Let these words of Jesus search you out today. Read them aloud so your ears can hear them. Remember, faith comes by hearing.

SING WITH ME

Today we will sing—you guessed it—"White Flag." It's in the playlist (www.christomlin.com/singwithme). Invite Jesus to take the song and lead you into deep surrender, a giving over of your will to Him.

HOW GREAT?

When is the last time you remember surrendering all to Jesus? How might His Gethsemane prayer—"not my will but yours be done"—become part of your ongoing, everyday life? How might a sense of surrendered abandonment to Jesus become a lifestyle for you rather than an occasional altar?

My Chains Are Gone

As most weekends go for me, I found myself at the airport headed to a city somewhere in the landscape of the US for what I hoped would be an amazing night of worship. As I arrived at my gate, I noticed an old familiar face I hadn't seen in quite a while. It was my mysterious friend from South Africa, Malcolm. I say mysterious because this guy has shown up in my life over the years during quite pivotal times for me, always with a word of wisdom. This chance—or better yet, divine—encounter would be no different. As we boarded the flight, our seats turned out to be in the same row together. What are the chances, right? We both had a laugh and looked at each other like, *What is happening right now?*

After the usual time of catching up, Mal said, "This is crazy running into you like this." I replied, "I know." He said, "No, what I mean is, I was in a conversation this weekend with some guys who were making a movie, and your name came up." I said, "My name? For a movie? Do they want me to star in the movie?" He replied with a polite "no" and then began to tell me about the movie called *Amazing Grace*, about the life of William Wilberforce. Seeing the blank look on my face, he showed me a short, trailer-like video about the giant changemaker who was Wilberforce. Talk about a worship-led life.

In the later part of the eighteenth century, Wilberforce had plans to go into the ministry but soon realized that maybe he could make an even greater impact and mark on the world by doing public service in the political realm. Over his life span, Wilberforce founded or co-founded some seventy-five organizations for the betterment of the world. He led movements like prison reform and started the first animal welfare society. He is best known as the leader of the movement for the abolition of slavery in England. In fact, Abraham Lincoln considered Wilberforce one of his great inspirations. Wilberforce spent most of his life fighting for the freedom of the enslaved. Stunningly, he died the day after learning of the government guarantee to pass the Slavery Abolition Act of 1833.

Malcolm went on, "The reason they are calling the movie *Amazing Grace* is because Wilberforce's mentor and ally was a man named John Newton." This name *did* ring a bell for me. Newton had penned the lyrics to what I consider probably the greatest song ever written. Yep— "Amazing Grace." Malcolm told me my name had come up because some people working on the movie wondered if I would be willing to write an add-on chorus to the hymn.

I immediately thought, *No, I am not going to be the punk who is accused of ruining the greatest song of all time.* I felt it was a no-win situation for me. Yet Malcolm pleaded, "Why don't you go read about how the hymn was written, and see if it doesn't inspire something in you?" I promised him I would do that but told him not to hold his breath.

Here's what I never knew: John Newton had been a slave trader for many years, steering the wheel of these dreadful ships of darkness across the Atlantic. Jesus radically saved Newton and transformed his life. He spent his latter years as an Anglican priest, speaking out against the cruel injustice of slavery and helping lead the charge for its abolition. In one his sermons, Newton wrote these words:

> Amazing grace how sweet the sound
> that saved a wretch like me
> I once was lost but now I'm found
> was blind but now I see.

There were many more verses alongside this one. Several made it into today's hymnals; other verses were lost to time. I had no idea this great song had been born out of the darkness of human slavery. In my research I made two interesting discoveries: First, I discovered that Newton did not write the "When we've been there ten thousand years" verse. Second, I found a "lost" verse—one dropped from the hymn in the 1900s:

> The earth shall soon dissolve like snow
> The sun forbear to shine

But God who called me here below
Will be forever mine.

In my research, I also read some of the testimonies of
slaves. Here's what blew me away: Despite their chains of
enslavement, they were among the most faith-filled people
in history. Because of this, they knew the freedom born of
heaven, flowing from the throne of God, by the blood of
Jesus Christ. Though bound by chains, they knew a freedom
their masters could not comprehend. At that point, I think I
heard the voice of Sir William Wallace in my ear, "They may
take our lives, but they can never take our freedom!" I sensed
the Lord was giving me the chorus. I sat down at the piano as
both lyrics and melody seemed to flow from heaven:

My chains are gone.
I've been set free.
My God, my Savior
Has ransomed me,
And like a flood
His mercy reigns;
Unending love,
Amazing grace.

The chains of human chattel slavery are an abomina-
tion, and we must never cease our mission to end it. We
need to be clear, though: human slavery exists because
humans are enslaved in the bondage of sin and darkness.
Think about it. The sex trade only exists because of the

unbridled cravings of lustful men and the covetous greed that fuels it. This invisible bondage of darkness leads to the physical chains of slavery.

THE BRIDGE

I wonder how you are assessing the state of your freedom in Jesus Christ. Jesus said, "If the Son sets you free, you will be free indeed" (John 8:36). The apostle Paul later wrote:

> *So I find this law at work: Although I want to do good, evil is right there with me. For in my inner being I delight in God's law; but I see another law at work in me, waging war against the law of my mind and making me a prisoner of the law of sin at work within me.* Romans 7:21–23

I want us to be honest with ourselves today. Are you "free indeed," or are you still held captive to the rogue power of sin even as a follower of Jesus?

SING WITH ME

I want us to sing this greatest hymn ever today, along with the tiny chorus we added in celebration. Pull up "Amazing Grace (My Chains are Gone)" on our playlist (www.christomlin.com/singwithme). I love, love, love Phil Wickham's "Living Hope," so let's sing that one today as well.

HOW GREAT?

How are you growing in freedom from the power of sin and the fear of death? In what ways is Jesus setting you free from sin, from yourself, from your fear of what others think of you? What seems impossible to be set free from at this time in your life? How might your faith increase, even by one degree, on this front?

11

The Wonderful Cross

There is a massive expanse of field just outside Memphis, Tennessee, known as Shelby Farms. We held a little gathering there back at the turn of the century—May 20, 2000, to be exact. Somewhere between thirty and forty thousand college students converged for a meeting called OneDay2000. Sponsored by Passion, it was billed as a sacred assembly, a day of worship and prayer for the awakening of a generation.

One of the things I loved about Passion in those early days was that they did not list or advertise the names of any preachers, presenters, or worship leaders. The only name was Jesus. Of course, back then it would not have helped to list any of our names, because most of us were brand-new to this work of leading worship. The list included David Crowder, Charlie Hall, Christy and Nathan Nockels, and this young, unknown upstart from England. You may have heard of him—Matt Redman.

I had a new song I wanted to release for the first time at OneDay. I called it "The Wonderful Cross" and wanted Matt to help me record it. Maybe you've heard it—a short chorus attached to the magisterial hymn from Isaac Watts, "When I Survey the Wondrous Cross."

As we introduced the song, none of us was prepared for what happened—which was one of the most compelling visions I have ever witnessed of what a worship-led life is all about. A time of confession and repentance gave way to a time of pardon and forgiveness. In the gathering clouds, I could sense the great cloud of witnesses gathering. It was worship at its best, transcending generations and cultures, traditional hymn colliding with modern chorus; Isaac Watts meets Matt Redman meets yours truly.

> When I survey the wondrous cross on which the
>   Prince of Glory died.

From the back of the field, several people began making their way to the stage. As they neared, it was apparent they were straining under the weight of a large wooden cross. As they made their way through the crowd, the decibel level of singing increased dramatically.

> My richest gain I count but loss and pour contempt
>   on all my pride.

As the cross came closer to the stage, people spontaneously left the crowd and began to follow in a kind of heavenly procession. The saints in glory were on their feet now, shouting, "Run!" and others from the far reaches of the field began running with reckless abandon, pursuing the cross.

See, from his head, his hands, his feet; sorrow and
love flow mingled down.

Singing was not enough. Tears were inadequate. Prayers could not contain it.

Did ever such love and sorrow meet or thorns com-
pose so rich a crown?

Calvary was emerging before our very eyes, and the response was extravagant.

Were the whole realm of nature mine, that were a
present far too small.

Women and men threw themselves at the foot of that cross, faces to the ground. Others pushed and pressed their way through the crowd just to touch it, as though it were the hem of His robe. Pride was shed like a dirty garment. Dignity was discarded. For a moment we resolved to know nothing but Jesus Christ and Him crucified.

Love so amazing, so divine, demands my soul, my
life, my all.
Oh the wonderful cross. Oh the wonderful cross.
Bids me come and die and find that I may
truly live.

Because of the cross, worship is not a straining toward heaven but an entry into it; not a remembrance of Calvary but a participation in it. Worship at its best is not an event but an encounter between heaven and earth. Beauty transforms shame. Glory transcends pain. Glorious life is birthed out of painful death at the wonderful cross. This is the very essence of the worship-led life. We are following Jesus, the ultimate worship leader, who led by laying down His life; the one who said "whoever wants to save their life will lose it, but whoever loses their life for me will find it" (Matthew 16:25)

> *For the message of the cross is foolishness to those who are perishing, but to us who are being saved it is the power of God.* 1 Corinthians 1:18

And what is the message of the cross?

> *But because of his great love for us, God, who is rich in mercy, made us alive with Christ even when we were dead in transgressions—it is by grace you have been saved.* Ephesians 2:4-5

> *God made him who had no sin to be sin for us, so that in him we might become the righteousness of God.* 2 Corinthians 5:21

> *Therefore, if anyone is in Christ, the new creation has come: The old has gone, the new is here!* 2 Corinthians 5:17

> *I have been crucified with Christ and I no longer live, but Christ lives in me. The life I now live in the body, I live by faith in the Son of God, who loved me and gave himself for me.* Galatians 2:20

The message of the cross is the secret to life: die before you die. Release your tight grip on your life and entrust yourself to the One who made you; who gave Himself for you; who knows you better than you know yourself; who delights in you; who has purposes and plans for your life.

> Love so amazing, so divine demands my soul, my life, my all.
> Oh, the wonderful cross. Oh, the wonderful cross. All who gather here by grace draw near and bless your name.

THE BRIDGE

I want us to take some time today and dwell on "the message of the cross," particularly as unfolded in those five verses of Scripture above. Here's the searching question I want each of us to ask: What is holding me back from going all in with Jesus?

Then, project yourself forward to the end of your life and ask, "Was it worth it to 'do it my way,' to hold my life back from Jesus and all He had designed for my life?"

SING WITH ME

Let's sing "The Wonderful Cross"—this freight train of a hymn (thank you, Isaac Watts)—along with the little caboose of a chorus I added. It's in the playlist (www.chris tomlin.com/singwithme). Pair this one with "Love Ran Red" for good measure today.

HOW GREAT?

Many of us are used to an empty and clean cross, but is the tomb that is empty. How might we survey the wondrous cross in all its fullness—see His head, His hands, His feet? How might you grow in your capacity to behold Jesus on the Cross more deeply—gazing upon the beauty of the Lord?

Jesus: Our Teacher

J ust as Jesus was His disciples' rabbi, He is our rabbi. A rabbi is a teacher. Jesus taught His disciples, but not like most of the teachers I have known. Don't hear me wrong. I have loved my teachers, except for that high school choir teacher who told me I couldn't sing and that I should choose another line of work (true story).

Most of my formal education was filled with what I would call an informational model. I was taught a lot of information and learned to master many subjects, but I wouldn't say it was transformational. If you are an athlete, you want to master your sport. If you are a doctor, you want to master everything about the human body. The problem comes when we try to take the informational educational model and bring it over into our life with God. It simply does not work with the worship-led life.

The worship-led life does not work by an informational model or even a traditional educational approach, for that matter. The worship-led life is a transformational model.

We see this model at work when we watch Jesus with His disciples. He is not teaching them to master a subject; rather, He is training them to be mastered by a subject. The subject is God Himself. It makes sense, doesn't it? The worship-led life is one of transformational learning whose goal and end is to be mastered by God. Remember what Jesus's disciples called Him? Master!

So if Jesus's approach to the worship-led life does not work by learning a lot of information, how does it work? Thanks for asking. It works not by information but by imitation and impartation. It is amazing how the first Christians were not called Christians. They were called simply people of "the Way."

Remember what Jesus said about Himself: "I am the way and the truth and the life. No one comes to the Father except through me" (John 14:6). When we follow the Way who is Jesus, we discover the Truth who is Jesus, and we are led into the Life who is Jesus. And the Life? Yes, the Life is the worship-led life.

So how does this really work? Let's take the example of prayer. One day Jesus's disciples came to Him with this request:

> *One day Jesus was praying in a certain place. When he finished, one of his disciples said to him, "Lord, teach us to pray, just as John taught his disciples."* Luke 11:1

For starters, notice how they observed Jesus "praying in a certain place." They were always watching Jesus. They were picking up on the ways of the Way. They were not learning by information but by observation. They noticed this pattern Jesus had of withdrawing to places by himself to pray. Here are a few examples from across the Gospels:

One of those days Jesus went out to a mountainside to pray, and spent the night praying to God. Luke 6:12

Yet the news about him spread all the more, so that crowds of people came to hear him and to be healed of their sicknesses. But Jesus often withdrew to lonely places and prayed. Luke 5:15-16

At daybreak, Jesus went out to a solitary place. The people were looking for him and when they came to where he was, they tried to keep him from leaving them. Luke 4:42

He withdrew about a stone's throw beyond them, knelt down and prayed, "Father, if you are willing, take this cup from me; yet not my will, but yours be done." An angel from heaven appeared to him and strengthened him. And being in anguish, he prayed more earnestly, and his sweat was like drops of blood falling to the ground. Luke 22:41–44

Jesus was with people constantly. He couldn't get away from them even when He tried. Still, we notice how their observation of Him brought them to a place of curiosity, and now their curiosity was turning into hunger. They were ready for imitation. They noticed how John had taught his disciples to pray. They wanted Jesus to teach them to pray in similar fashion. I've always wondered what John must have taught his disciples. Clearly, Jesus's teaching would be next-level. Those disciples knew they were about to get the secret sauce of Jesus. Let's get it straight from the Bible:

And when you pray, do not be like the hypocrites, for they love to pray standing in the synagogues and on the street corners to be seen by others. Truly I tell you, they have received their reward in full. Matthew 6:5

Jesus, the Way, teaches them the way. It is not the way of the religious elite. He's telling them that the people everyone thinks are the prayer leaders aren't the real prayer leaders at all. Prayer is not a public performance. It is not a show. It is not about impressing people. The disciples have noticed how Jesus's prayer life has happened not on the street corners but in the secret places. He is telling them they will not find the real worship leaders on the street corners, because they will be spending their time with God in the secret places. The worship-led life is a secret and hidden life. It is not about impressing others. It's not about others at all. It is about God alone. Hear him out:

But when you pray, go into your room, close the door and pray to your Father, who is unseen. Then your Father, who sees what is done in secret, will reward you. Matthew 6:6

Jesus, the Way, is showing them the way. As he does this, He is revealing the Truth. Prayer is the portal between the seen world and the unseen reality. Unless it happens in secret, prayer can seem like a show. Prayer is not meant to be the ongoing punctuation of our lives but the sentence itself. Prayer is an ongoing, hidden, intimate conversation with the living God. And also this—God rewards secret prayer. He continues the impartation of revelation:

> *And when you pray, do not keep on babbling like pagans, for they think they will be heard because of their many words. Do not be like them, for your Father knows what you need before you ask him.*
> Matthew 6:7–8

This is revolutionary. How much time and how many words have I spent telling God all about my needs? In fact, if I'm honest, I still do my fair share of presenting my needs to God. Jesus said He already knows our needs. Look how much time this frees up to simply worship God. It shows me just how easy it is for me to turn prayer into a me-centered activity. Jesus wants us to be freed up for God-centered adoration.

In all these ways, we are seeing how Jesus is not teaching for information. He is training for transformation. He is not leading us to master a subject or a practice. He is leading us in the way of being mastered by God. He is not working according to our typical educational model. He is walking us into the mysterious way of imitation becoming impartation.

THE BRIDGE

I want to point out a power verse today. It is packed with revelation and yet so plainly and simply stated:

Rejoice always, pray continually, give thanks in all circumstances; for this is God's will for you in Christ Jesus. 1 Thessalonians 5:16–18

Rejoice always. Pray continually. Give thanks.

Have you noticed how football quarterbacks these days have little books on their forearms? They have all the plays a coach might call so they can make sure they get it right. Well, God's Word is our playbook. This is how we were made to live. Rejoice always. Pray continually. Give thanks. Let's run those plays all day long.

SING WITH ME

I wrote and recorded a song a few years back titled, simply, "Jesus." Can we sing this one today? It's on the playlist (www.christomlin.com/singwithme). As we sing it, let the Holy Spirit unfurl His life like a banner that encircles and enfolds us, going before us and behind us. I'd like us to also pull up Pat Barrett's "The Way (New Horizon)" and sing it out today.

HOW GREAT?

How are you experiencing a fresh yearning for a new and deeper way of prayer? What kinds of intentions is the Holy Spirit forming in you today? How might you take a step to respond to these promptings?

13

Good Good Father

As we learned in the last entry, Jesus (the Way) has been teaching us the Truth and is about to break forth into the Life. He uses a revolutionary word to describe the very nature of God—a word that becomes a doorway into the very life of prayer. That word is *Father*.

The Bible offers us literally hundreds of names for God. He is called Elohim, Adonai, and El Shaddai. He is Jehovah Jireh (provider), Jehovah Rapha (healer), Jehovah Shalom (peace), Jehova Nissi (banner), Jehovah Rohi (shepherd), and the list continues.

We see God imaged throughout Scripture as a mighty and sovereign king and as a just and righteous judge. All of these names reveal a major quality of God or indicate something that God does. As king, God reigns. As judge, God rules. God also provides, heals, gives peace, and so on. This is what is so revolutionary about the way Jesus prayed. He didn't use any of the many names we have for God throughout the Scriptures. Instead, He used a term hardly ever seen or used in the Old Testament. After telling us to go into a room, close the door, and let go of our many words (Matthew 6:6), He told us how to greet God—you might say He gave us the name of all names for our God.

You know it—a name of profound endearment: *Father.*

Even as I am writing this, I am realizing something. Jesus is not trying to teach us something about God. He is revealing to us something about His relationship to God. We didn't really know God as Father until we knew God had a Son. Here, the Son of God invites us into the most profound relationship on earth. He doesn't invite us into the relationship of a loyal subject to their king—though this relationship is true. He doesn't invite us into the relationship of a guilty sinner with a merciful judge—though this relationship is real. He invites us into the relationship of sons and daughters with a loving father.

It gets even better. Jesus is not saying, "I want you to pray like I pray so you can have a relationship with God like I have a relationship with God." This is not instructive teaching. It is invitational. Jesus is inviting us into His very relationship with His Father. It's why he says "Our Father." *Our* doesn't just mean me and all y'all. It means Jesus and us. Jesus is bringing us on the inside of His relationship with His Father. He is now "Our Father."

And this, my friends, is a good, good father.

Here is the hard part for so many: they did not grow up with a good, good father. Many of you grew up and even suffered at the hands of broken and unhealed parents. You experienced abuse and neglect, and this imprinted on your deepest self and keeps you from believing that God could be a good Father. Your earliest experiences also led you to believe things about yourself that aren't true—like maybe that you aren't lovable or worthy of love.

I want you to know how sorry I am for this. This is never what God intended for you. Sadly, you are in good company in this me-driven world. While it is not an excuse, the broken ways of our fathers and mothers tend to come from the broken ways of *their* fathers and mothers. We are caught and even trapped in what is known as generational sin. It keeps getting passed down. Here's the good news we discover in the worship-led life: Jesus breaks the line of generational sin. He restores us to a relationship with our good, good Father. He heals our broken hearts and sets us free. Every time we pray to Our Father, the healing deepens.

One day when Jesus was teaching the crowds, He said this:

> *Which of you, if your son asks for bread, will give him a stone? Or if he asks for a fish, will give him a snake? If you, then, though you are evil, know how to give good gifts to your children, how much more will your Father in heaven give good gifts to those who ask him! Matthew 7:9–11*

Luke records Jesus as saying, "How much more will your Father in heaven give the Holy Spirit to those who ask him!" (11:13). This is the very best gift of all, because it is the gift of His presence in the deepest place of our lives. Watch what happens when He gives us this gift:

For those who are led by the Spirit of God are the children of God. The Spirit you received does not make you slaves, so that you live in fear again; rather, the Spirit you received brought about your adoption to sonship. And by him we cry, "Abba, Father." The Spirit himself testifies with our spirit that we are God's children.
Romans 8:14–16

This is why I love the song "Good Good Father" so much and why I think it touched the hearts of so many. This is the place of our deepest brokenness. As Jesus introduces us to our good, good Father, it becomes the place of our deepest healing.

THE BRIDGE

Did you catch that little phrase in Romans 8: *Abba Father?* This takes "Our Father" to the next level. In the Middle East, both in ancient times and today, this word *Abba* is the intimate and endearing way children address their fathers. The English equivalent is something like *Dadda* or *Daddy.* I want to encourage you to try speaking to God with these two words, *Abba Father.* It may feel awkward at first, but give it time. I can tell you what He will say back to you: "My beloved."

SING WITH ME

I would love for us to sing "Good Good Father" today. Pull it up on the playlist (www.christomlin.com/singwithme)

and give it a go. And let me introduce you to another little-known song of mine that can lead us today: "My Beloved." It was a hidden track way back on the *Hello Love* record. I've put it in the playlist.

HOW GREAT?

How are you discovering God as a good, good Father? How do the wounds from your earthly father and/or mother hold you back from relating to God in this way? Will you open yourself up to the healing work of the Holy Spirit to restore your broken image of God?

My Reward Is Giving Glory to You

"Create in me a pure heart, O God, and renew a steadfast spirit within me" **(Psalm 51:10).**

We all remember those days at the dawn of 2020, when everything began to come undone around us. The strange sickness of COVID-19 swept the world, striking down millions in its wake. Everything shut down. We learned again to treasure what mattered most: family, friends, faith, and life itself. As churches were forced to cancel gatherings for weekly worship, one of the unexpected gifts of the shutdown became "Home Church." Through those days God brought us back to a pure place of simplicity in His presence. He kept bringing me back to one of the

songs of my growing up years: "O Lord, You're Beautiful."
Maybe you remember it too.

> O Lord you're beautiful
> Your face is all I seek,
> And when your eyes are on this child
> Your grace abounds to me.

Sunday after Sunday, for a whole year, I would grab
my guitar and we would sing this song together as a family.
I can still hear the sweet voices of my little girls singing,
"and when your eyes are on this child, your grace abounds
to me." I was reminded of the legendary songwriter of this
simple yet profound song, Keith Green. Keith's home, Last
Days Ministries, was located just fifteen miles from where
I grew up in Texas. Keith and his wife, Melody, showed us
the real shape of a worship-led life.

They were trailblazers. Keith was a prophetic voice with
a piano. He was famous for coming home from tour stops
with new people on the bus who he had picked up at his
concerts—people who needed something in their lives,
whether it be healing, discipleship, or just food and shelter. The Last Days compound was legendary around our
area for housing so many of these Jesus people. Shockingly,
Keith's life was cut short at just twenty-eight years old in an
airplane accident there on the property.

Maybe one of the most profound things I gleaned from
Keith was from the book about his life, *No Compromise*,
which was taken from his journals and written by his wife,
Melody, and David Hazard. Keith journaled about how he

MY REWARD IS GIVING GLORY TO YOU

had made music an idol, and how his making music for God had become more important than God Himself. He committed to lay it down and not touch the piano until God spoke to him and he felt the freedom to play again. This suspension of music carried on for weeks that turned into months until, as Melody wrote, she heard the startling sound of piano keys being played in the middle of the night. There she found Keith pouring his heart out to God. He had returned to the simplicity of a worship-led life— that simple place of purity in the presence of Jesus.

> O Lord, please light the fire
> that once burned bright and clear
> replace the Lamp of my first love
> that burns with holy fear

Fast-forward now to the days following the global pandemic. As I approached the record label about the project we would call *Always*, I told them the first song I wanted to record was "O Lord, You're Beautiful." I remember saying to my team, "I know I didn't write this one, but I've sung it every Sunday for the past year with my family, and it has done something deep inside my soul. It has brought me back to a holy place of simplicity in the presence of God. I think it may do the same for others."

My producer suggested Gordon Mote, a piano player I had never met but knew by his incredible reputation. Blind from birth, Gordon is one of the most gifted piano players and artists you will ever hear. I'll never forget meeting him that morning at the studio for the first time and saying, "I don't know if you are familiar with the song, 'O Lord, You're Beautiful,' by Keith Green, but I would love to record it with you today." He instantly lit up and said, "Oh yes, one of my absolute favorites of all time . . . would somebody help me get to a piano; I am ready to go."

I mention this because when you hear my recording from the *Always* album, the piano on that song was one take—we did not rehearse. Gordon said, "Let's just hit record and see what happens." We kept it just as it was. It was breathtaking. I felt the wind of God's Spirit in the room so strongly. Of course, I had to resing my part, because I was sobbing by the end of the first run-through. I was overwhelmed all at once with the words I was singing, the journey this song had taken me on during the past year with my family, and my own heart. Watching Gordon pour out his gift on the piano sent me over the top.

I was particularly moved by a part of the song I had never noticed that much before. God took the bridge-like section to deeply stir my heart. Hear its prophetic charge:

> I want to take your word and shine it all around
> first help me just to live it Lord
> and when I'm doing well
> help me to never seek a crown
> for my reward is giving glory to you

Those words, "My reward is giving glory to you," resonated in the deepest part of my heart. This is the essence of the worship-led life, isn't it? It's what I want said of my own life. I look around my office and see the plaques on the wall and the awards and little statues scattered all around. In my career, I have been blessed to receive many accolades for my music, and I am grateful for all of them. To me, though, they are markers that somehow God has used my music to touch people—to give them a voice to worship Him and the soundtrack to live it out. But truly, my ultimate reward is giving glory back to the One who gave me these gifts. Any crown that I may receive, I will one day lay at His feet.

THE BRIDGE

Keith Green also wrote the song "Create in Me a Clean Heart," based on the lyrics of Psalm 51. Dwell deeply on these verses below. Let the words lead you to honest confession and humble repentance. Invite the Holy Spirit to lead you to a place of simplicity and purity before Jesus.

> *Create in me a pure heart, O God, and renew a steadfast spirit within me. Do not cast me from your presence or take your Holy Spirit from me. Restore to me the joy of your salvation and grant me a willing spirit, to sustain me.* Psalm 51:10–12

SING WITH ME

Queue up "O Lord You're Beautiful" on our Worship-Led Life Playlist (www.christomlin.com/singwithme) and spend some time in ministry to the Lord today. Let the lyrics of this powerful song wash over you before singing along. Jump in when you are ready to lift your voice.

HOW GREAT?

How are you sensing Jesus "re-lighting" the fire that once burned bright and clear? How is the desire deepening in you to be restored to your first love? How might you make an altar called "First Love" today and return to the Lord with all your heart?

PART III

OUTWARD

Others

I t was Christmas Eve, 1910. Almost blind and very sick, William Booth was now in his 80s. One thing he looked forward to most was the annual convention of the upstart organization he had founded to do good around the world. But this year he couldn't make it to the convention. Instead, he thought he would send a telegram for one of his men to read that could kick off the gathering.

Booth searched for the words to encourage the men and women working so hard to help the poor and needy during the winter cold and holidays. In those days, telegrams charged by the word, and Mr. Booth wanted every possible penny to help as many people as he could—he didn't want to waste too much on a piece of paper. After thinking long and hard, he wrote out what he would declare as his life mission and the mission of his organization. When his colleague stood in front of this growing team of world changers, he announced that their fearless leader was in no health to be present. Obviously, this was a massive disappointment to all. However, he had a telegram from Mr. Booth to read it to everyone. He opened the telegram and read it:

"Others."

Yes, just one word. William Booth said all he needed to say with just single word. I love it. Others, period. Maybe you're wondering about this upstart organization? The Salvation Army!

A worship-led life is a road-tested life, and the test is the movement toward other people. A worship-led life is about others. Mother Teresa said it bluntly: "A life not lived for others is not a life." The me-driven world is all about . . . well . . . me.

A friend of mine once gave me some advice about breaking the ice with strangers in a conversation. "Just ask questions," he said, "and get them talking about themselves. It's their favorite subject." Funny, but true. You know you have met your match in conversation when someone keeps trying to turn the subject around to you as you are trying to keep the focus on them. It's a good picture of Romans 12:10, which says, "Be devoted to one another in love. Honor one another above yourselves."

One of our core family values is held in the three-word phrase, "I am third." It comes from a book by the same title from the legendary football player Gale Sayers. The phrase was popularized by the well-known Missouri-based sports camp Kanakuk (a place where my wife, Lauren, was a Kickapoo princess, by the way). God is first. Others are second. I am third. You will hear Lauren and me using this phrase—"I am third"—around the house with our girls all the time. The truth? It's as much for us as it is for them.

Living with an others orientation is a lifelong journey. And I'm not sure we can ever completely master it.

Here is a core life passage about what it looks like to live a worship-led life:

> *Through Jesus, therefore, let us continually offer to God a sacrifice of praise—the fruit of lips that openly profess his name. And do not forget to do good and to share with others, for with such sacrifices God is pleased.* Hebrews 13:15–16

"Through Jesus"—this is the only way worship happens.

"Let us continually offer to God a sacrifice of praise— the fruit of lips that openly profess his name." It would be easy to stop there. After all, this is mostly how we think about worship, isn't it? Praising God. It's what I have given my life's work to do. This is why my band gets on a bus and travels from town to town, sets up, and plays our hearts out night after night. There is nothing like the sound of people praising God.

But the Scripture doesn't end with a great sound of praise. Look at the next verse: "And do not forget to do good and to share with others, for with such sacrifices God is pleased."

There it is: *others*. A worship-led life is about both song and service; about loving God and neighbor; about the seamless movement between the sanctuary and the streets. In other words, how can we gather and sing and not be led to action for those around us?

Many years ago I had a vivid dream I knew was from the Lord. You should know this just doesn't happen to me.

I pray for such things, but rarely if ever do they happen. I pray for songs in the night—to wake up and have the song. I once heard that Paul McCartney dreamed the song "Yesterday" in its entirety. Then he woke up and wrote it all down. I'm not sure if it's true, but that would be amazing. I'll keep praying.

This dream was different. I knew it was a message from the Lord. It was one of those panic dreams we've all had in some way or another. In the dream I had forgotten my own concert. I was in a panic. I rushed to my car and sped to the venue. I vividly remember coming to a red light. Totally stressed out, I looked to my left and could see a football stadium in the distance filled with people gathered for my concert. I could hear my band playing on the stage.

I could not believe I had forgotten this night. It's interesting because it's been one of my "dreams" to play in a stadium, and I never have. At the same red light, I looked to my right, and there in the middle of the street was a tiny baby—naked, abandoned, terrified, and screaming. I kept looking back to the left at the stadium and then to the right at the baby. I can still feel the dilemma from within the dream: *What do I do? I have to get to this concert, but how can I go and sing these songs to God while leaving this precious baby in the street?* I jumped out of the car and grabbed the baby. Then I got back in the car, sat the baby on my lap, and suddenly woke up. I sat straight up in the bed and wondered, *What is the meaning of this dream?* At that time I had no children, but I knew God was speaking to me.

That dream has stayed with me, and over the past few years its meaning has become both more obvious and more clear: take the baby to the concert; our worship is not complete until it finds its way into the street. The worship-led life is so much more than songs and singing. It is about our eyes being opened to see the great need around us and our hearts being broken to meet those people and needs.

THE BRIDGE

The biblical prophets come down pretty hard on singing in church while ignoring people in need in the streets. Take a look at how Amos, the farmer prophet, put it:

> *Away with the noise of your songs! I will not listen to the music of your harps. But let justice roll on like a river, righteousness like a never-failing stream!* Amos 5:23–24

Meditate on this text today. Let its words search you out as you invite the Holy Spirit to reintegrate your love for God with your love for others and make your worship complete.

SING WITH ME

I wrote a song many years ago that I want to dig back out to sing with you today: "This Is Our God." It is a song of the Lord's compassion meant both to comfort and to challenge us. Let's sing it in a contemplative spirit today.

HOW GREAT?

Have you considered how loving and serving others is as much an act of worship as singing and praising God? How is your life being led in worship as relates to serving other people these days? How might you grow in this area?

Salt of the Earth

I am from Grand Saline, a small country town in East Texas. It's funny how people often refer to people who live in small towns as "salt of the earth" type people. This is quite literal when it comes to my town. Grand Saline means "Big Salt." It gets better: our little town sits atop a massive salt dome. In fact, it is known as the Morton Salt Mine. Yep, those boxes of salt with the little girl in the yellow dress with an umbrella—straight out of my town. We went to the same elementary school (just kidding!).

My brothers and I loved to take our little Honda ATV with the throttle wide open across those massive white fields of salt. All the men who work in the mine drive old cars, because they rust out every few years. I remember seeing all those little rust buckets driving through town every afternoon about 4 p.m. when the day shift was over. Grand Saline is home to the Salt Festival, the Salt Rodeo, and even the Salt Queen. I cut my musical teeth playing songs at several events during these gatherings over the years.

Years ago, I read an article saying there's enough salt under my little town to supply the whole earth for the next three hundred thousand years. Yes, with a population of three thousand and a three hundred thousand–year supply of salt, we can back up the claim as "salt of the earth" kind of people. I wonder if you can guess our favorite verse from the Bible? Yep! It's Matthew 5:13:

> *You are the salt of the earth. But if the salt loses its saltiness, how can it be made salty again? It is no longer good for anything, except to be thrown out and trampled underfoot.*

Scholars have long debated just what exactly Jesus meant when He coined this most famous phrase: *salt of the earth.* For me, it's pretty simple. I just think about the people of Grand Saline, Texas, and so many more I have met over the years. I think about my mom and dad and the little pharmacy they ran down on Main Street. I think about Paul and Melanie Roberts, who spent their time off from building their own business to build faith in me and other youth in our little church. I think about my Papaw, who taught me to fish and water ski, and how every meal began with a good joke and a faithful prayer. I think about my teachers and coaches who shaped me in those early years. For my money, when Jesus said, "You are the salt of the earth," that's who He was talking about.

Salt is common. Salt heals. Salt flavors. Salt purifies and cleanses. Recent studies have shown that ions emitted from salt purify the air. Salt rooms are now turning up across the country, where engineers have created generators that mimic the effects of Himalayan salt in the air. The idea is to relax in these room and breathe in the salty air. This has proven to reduce congestion and help greatly with allergies, asthma, and other breathing ailments.

I love the story about Jesus after He rose from the dead—the one where He was meeting with His disciples and breathed on them, saying, "Receive the Holy Spirit" (John 20:22). When we receive the Holy Spirit, we are inhaling the breath of God. It stands to reason, then, that when we exhale, we are breathing out the breath of God on others. As salt of the earth people, what if our presence in a room makes it easier for others to breathe freely? What a thought—as we walk out the worship-led life, we become air purifiers.

Salt is well-known for its healing power. Since ancient times, people have flocked to the Dead Sea in Israel to bathe there. I have a surfer friend who speaks of this healing power as well. He tells me time and again how he loves to surf because the salt water seems to cure whatever is ailing him. You have heard the saying, "Don't rub salt in a wound." In ancient times, salt was mixed with honey and applied to wounds for healing. Yes, it stings, but doesn't healing always involve some discomfort? In the process, salt also acts as a preservative.

Jesus said, "You will know the truth, and the truth will set you free" (John 8:32). Can we be honest? The truth can be salty. Sometimes it burns. It always ultimately heals. When we live a worship-led life, our presence can at times make others uncomfortable. When we live our lives as though Jesus is in the room, others become aware—sometimes uncomfortably and sometimes painfully—that Jesus is actually in the room.

Finally, salt enhances flavor. I especially love this idea. So many people think the worship-led life can only be lived in a monastery somewhere on the side of a mountain. They misunderstand both real life and monasteries. Many carry the misguided notion that a life lived for God is a boring life, leading to the death of our desires and passion for living. Nothing could be further from the truth. Jesus said the exact opposite: "The thief comes only to steal and kill and destroy; I have come that they may have life, and have it to the full" (John 10:10).

Jesus doesn't bring blandness but brilliance. Actually, salt doesn't *add* flavor; it intensifies the flavor already there. Salt tastes like . . . well . . . salt, but when you put salt on a steak, the steak tastes more like steak than ever before. Add more salt to tortilla chips, and all of a sudden the salsa starts singing on key. The me-driven world is filled with all kinds of strategies and substances to somehow add more and more flavors to our lives. People are ever striving to craft and create their identities by enhancing their appearance or adding to their possessions or going for more and more experiences, as though this could satisfy their deepest longings. Rather than bringing out and accentuating what is most deeply there, all of this activity covers it and masks the true reality. There's a term for it: artificial flavors. In contrast, salt reveals and brings out the flavor already there.

This is how it is with Jesus. He alone sees who we most truly are, because He made us. He wants to bring out every bit of our flavor and share it with others. The amazing thing

about a person becoming their real self is how it gives everyone else around the permission and freedom to be their real
selves too.

Salt purifies. Salt heals. Salt flavors. Notice how all of
those things are outwardly oriented toward others. When
Jesus says we are the salt of the earth, He is not calling us
to be more religious. He's inviting us to become more real
and, in becoming more real, to become more relational.
He's not asking us to be impressive or sophisticated but to
become more humble. That's it—more humble. Humility
is not making less of yourself; it is making more of others.
It's not putting yourself down; it's lifting others up. That's
what salt of the earth kind of people do. I hope someday
someone will say of me, "That Chris Tomlin, he was a salt
of the earth kind of guy!"

THE BRIDGE

Over the years, I've learned a simple lesson: we tend to
treat others like we treat ourselves. And we treat ourselves
like we believe, deep down, God treats us. That's why the
worship-led life begins there—with how God treats us. I
want us to remember our baptism today and those words
the Father spoke over us. They are the same unconditional,
irrevocable words He spoke over His Son at His baptism
(Matthew 3:17):

> You are my son/daughter.
> You are my beloved.
> With you, I am well pleased.

Whatever it takes, I want you to get this. When you finally believe this—really believe this—everything will change. Will you read it aloud over yourself today? Will you speak it for God over yourself? Invite someone close to speak it over you for God. Return the favor to them. Of all the words of God in the Word of God, this just may be the saltiest. It will purify, heal, flavor, and bless you to do the same for others.

SING WITH ME

I want us to sing the song "Jesus Loves Me" today. Not the children's version, though you can sing that one, too, if you're feeling it. This is the song from the *Love Ran Red* record. It's the salty song we need for the day.

HOW GREAT?

Salt heals. Salt flavors. Salt purifies and cleanses. Which one of these qualities most resonates with your life? How does your presence serve as a healing presence to others? A flavoring presence? A purifying presence? A cleansing presence?

17

God of This City

Over the decades I have been on the road leading worship, I have seen, heard, and experienced many things. I remember one particular night in Belfast, Northern Ireland. The event was a bit of a festival with several worship bands lined up for the day. I was excited to be included. It is always a blessing to lead the musically spirited Irish in worship.

On this night I found myself in a place pretty common in my life—a backstage dressing room. While every gathering and event is distinctive, every dressing room pretty much looks the same. It's usually a musty locker room with bad fluorescent lighting. We try to vibe up the mood by bringing in some lamps and hanging string lights. I remember this dressing room because of the way Daniel, my guitar player, crashed through the door with great excitement: "Did you just hear that song?!" He told me he'd just heard one of the best, most inspired songs he'd heard in a long while. It had come from the band known as Bluetree. I remember how he described the song as unlike any other song he'd ever heard.

The band had just finished their set, so we connected with them as they hopped off the stage. Daniel quickly asked the lead singer, Aaron Boyd, about the song. Aaron said, "Yeah, the song is called 'God of This City,' and I could send you a demo copy if you want."

As I listened to the song, it had the same effect on me that it'd had on Daniel. I put it on repeat and couldn't stop listening. There was something so captivating, so heartfelt, and so hopeful about this song. Right about this same time, we were planning our first-ever world tour with the college movement I was part of called Passion. I knew this was a "for such a time as this" song. You just know it when a song carries something special. I sensed what it would mean to sing these profound words in city after city across the world. I asked Aaron if we could be part of stewarding the gift of their song, singing it on the tour and later recording it. He graciously agreed. Then he told us the story of how the song came to be. It became obvious to me why this song was so special.

Aaron's band was given the opportunity to travel to Thailand to share their music and to minister to people. They went to Pattaya, a city of oppressive darkness, best known for being the world's hub for the human trafficking of young girls. In my mind, it just doesn't get any darker than this. One night his band was asked if they wanted to play at a bar on one of these seedy streets. I loved Aaron's response: "Of course we do!" I remember him telling me, "So here we were on the stage where young girls were forced to dance, only we were leading worship. No one knew any of the songs until we started playing Matt Redman's 'Blessed Be Your Name,' at which point a few drunk guys in the back began to hold up their drinks and sway and sing."

Nearing tears now, Aaron said, "Then it happened. As I looked over the crowd and thought of the dark hopelessness in the streets and across the city, my heart began to break, and I began to spontaneously sing out this prayer to God:

> You're the God of this city.
> You're the King of these people.
> You're the Lord of this nation.
> You are.
>
> You're the light in the darkness.
> You're the hope to the hopeless.
> You're the peace to the restless.
> You are.
>
> There is no one like our God.
> There is no one like our God.
>
> For greater things have yet to come
> and greater things are still to be done in this city."

Aaron said the whole song just flowed out like a prophetic declaration right there on the stage. I say it often: sometimes you are a songwriter, and other times you are a song-receiver. Aaron received the gift of this song on that night. It became both a shield of faith and a sabre of light cutting through the darkness. The purity of the Spirit of

God fell and covered the stage that had supported so much darkness. Is it any wonder how and why this song gripped us with such power? It still does all these years later. The song came straight from heaven. It feels a bit like Isaiah 58 put to melody:

> *Your people will rebuild the ancient ruins and will raise up the age-old foundations; you will be called Repairer of Broken Walls, Restorer of Streets with Dwellings.* Isaiah 58:12

It got me thinking about our songs as our lives. The songs we sing represent our hearts and our hopes. We sing many songs of transcendent glory. We sing even more songs of sanctifying deliverance. We sing fewer songs of prophetic mission. "God of This City" is one of those songs. It is one thing to let our songs lead us into the streets, where we must go. A song of prophetic mission is of another order entirely. The Spirit can take a prophetic song of mission and bring the streets into the sanctuary. These kinds of songs don't inspire mission projects. They beget Kingdom movements. That's it! Songs of prophetic mission become stories of prophetic movement.

Songs like this have inspired a new generation of abolitionists to take to the highways and the byways to end human slavery in our time. I am proud of how my dear friend and mentor and founder of Passion, Louie Giglio, along with his wife, Shelley, have invested so much into rescuing present-day slaves from the darkness of evil and restoring them by the Light who is Jesus.

Those who walk out the worship-led life are at the forefront of transforming streets into sanctuaries. I love the way the prophet Isaiah put it in his bold song of prophetic mission:

> *They will rebuild the ancient ruins and restore the places long devastated; they will renew the ruined cities that have been devastated for generations.*
> Isaiah 61:4

> For greater things have yet to come
> and greater things are still to be done in this city

Songs like this one don't come from working out melodies and lyrics in normal writing sessions. Lives like this don't come from résumé-building and carefully made strategic plans. They come from the wholesale abandonment of the me-driven world and utter consecration of our lives to our worship leader, Jesus. The test of a worship-led life is not the upward and inward but the outward, which is the life lived for others.

THE BRIDGE

I want us to reflect on one of the most pivotal texts in all of Scripture. I see it as the ultimate prophecy of the worship-led life. It comes from Isaiah 61 and actually precedes the verse shared above:

> *The Spirit of the Sovereign LORD is on me, because the LORD has anointed me to proclaim good news*

to the poor. He has sent me to bind up the broken-hearted, to proclaim freedom for the captives and release from darkness for the prisoners, to proclaim the year of the LORD's favor and the day of vengeance of our God, to comfort all who mourn, and provide for those who grieve in Zion—to bestow on them a crown of beauty instead of ashes, the oil of joy instead of mourning, and a garment of praise instead of a spirit of despair. They will be called oaks of righteousness, a planting of the LORD for the display of his splendor. Isaiah 61:1–3

This is the bridge from the sanctuary to the streets. I want us to build this bridge with our lives. It captures the outward movement of the life we are after—the life for others. I want you to scribe it down into your journal today. Let the Spirit lead you in deciding where to break the lines, in determining which words to capitalize and set apart. I want you to dwell deep in this text today, tomorrow, and the day after that—until the text is dwelling deep in you.

SING WITH ME

Queue up "God of This City" on our Worship-Led Life Playlist (www.christomlin.com/singwithme) and spend some time singing this prophetic declaration today. This is a song for the road, so take it out wherever you go today. Sing it loudly where you can and under your breath where you can't, but sing it like a prayer of declaration everywhere you go.

HOW GREAT?

How might you sing this song, "God of This City," and others like it as a song of prophetic declaration over your city? How about your neighborhood? How are you growing in your boldness as an agent of Jesus to others in your everyday life? Are you looking for everyday ways to "bind up the brokenhearted?"

God of Angel Armies

The me-driven world runs on the rails of fear and stands on the foundation of insecurity. Can we be honest? That is why we focus on ourselves. We are afraid. We are insecure. We don't believe there is enough for us all. We have to stake our claim, strive to make our own name, as we ever play the comparison game.

The worship-led life soars on the wings of faith, lives in the assurance of abundance, and runs free in the fields of faith. Our security is rooted at the foot of the cross, indeed at the very feet of our Lord Jesus. Our treasure is in heaven, and it is our Father's delight to give us the kingdom.

Allow me to draw out the contrast with a good old-fashioned Old Testament Bible story.

2 Kings 6:8 says, "Now the king of Aram was at war with Israel. After conferring with his officers, he said, 'I will set up my camp in such and such a place.'"

In those days, as in these, to oppose God's people was to oppose God Himself. Time and time again, the

Lord sovereignly revealed the plans of the King of Aram to His prophet, Elisha. And Elisha relayed those plans to the king of Israel. Time and time again, the Israelites eluded, upstaged, and upended the Arameans. The story continues:

> *This enraged the king of Aram. He summoned his officers and demanded of them, "Tell me! Which of us is on the side of the king of Israel?"*
>
> *"None of us, my lord the king," said one of his officers, "but Elisha, the prophet who is in Israel, tells the king of Israel the very words you speak in your bedroom."*
>
> *"Go, find out where he is," the king ordered, "so I can send men and capture him." The report came back: "He is in Dothan." Then he sent horses and chariots and a strong force there. They went by night and surrounded the city.*
>
> *When the servant of the man of God got up and went out early the next morning, an army with horses and chariots had surrounded the city. "Oh no, my lord! What shall we do?" the servant asked.*
>
> *"Don't be afraid," the prophet answered. "Those who are with us are more than those who are with them."*
>
> *And Elisha prayed, "Open his eyes, LORD, so that he may see." Then the LORD opened the servant's eyes, and he looked and saw the hills full of horses and chariots of fire all around Elisha.* 2 Kings 6:11–17

This, of course, is the story behind the song "God of Angel Armies." The me-driven world runs on the rails of fear. The worship-led life runs on the fuel of faith. Four of Jesus's favorite words are, "Do not be afraid." On the night He would give Himself up for us, as He was being arrested in the Garden of Gethsemane, Jesus famously said, "Do you think I cannot call on my Father, and he will at once put at my disposal more than twelve legions of angels?" (Matthew 26:53). For the record, that comes to 720,000 angels. Try to imagine that. The God of Angel Armies always wins, even when it looks like He loses.

A few years back I encountered a faith giant I will remember as long as I live. I arrived late to a conference on Bible translation. Standing in the lobby, while waiting to check into my room, I ran into a longtime friend. He grabbed me and said, "I love that I just ran into you because there is someone I want you to meet." He introduced me to a pastor who had just spoken at the session I'd missed. This humble man from Syria began to tell me his story, and once again I knew I was in the presence of one of the princes of the kingdom of heaven on earth.

He explained to me that he had grown up in an Islamic village and Muslim family, yet Jesus had begun to come to him in dreams. Night after night Jesus would appear, and every time He would say the same thing: "Follow me." This pastor knew nothing at all of Jesus but was strangely certain it was Him. One morning he awoke and decided today was the day—the day he would say yes to Jesus's invitation.

That decision would cost him pretty much everything: his family, his job, his friends, the whole world as he knew it. His own brothers told him he must renounce Jesus or they would kill him in the public square of the village. One of the brothers gave him the date: the upcoming Friday. He had until Friday to renounce Jesus or his life was over. Beaming with humility, this pastor looked me in the eye and said, "I knew Jesus was my Savior, and whatever happened on that Friday was up to God, but I would not renounce Jesus."

Then he whispered, "Thursday night, the night before, my brother died in his sleep."

He stared at me, letting the gravity of it all sink in. Then he continued, explaining how he planted a small house church in his village. "I live every single day as if it is my last day," he told me as he pulled a picture from his wallet—a photograph of the burial plot he's purchased for himself and his wife. He lives without fear, knowing that at any moment he could lose his life because of his faith. What a picture of a worship-led life!

Meanwhile, the friend who had introduced me to this Syrian pastor was still standing there. Out of nowhere my friend asked him, "Have you ever heard of Christian music or know of any songs?" I recoiled, thinking to myself, *What kind of question is that in the midst of a conversation like this?* I braced for an embarrassing moment. The pastor shook his head and said no. I was quietly relieved. He continued telling us absolute miracle stories of what God was doing in his village in Syria.

After a few minutes, though, the pastor paused and said, "Actually, I do know one Christian song—one song on my phone that I sing every morning. It's my song of faith before I go out to share Jesus with my people." He looked and me and said:

> "I know who goes before me,
> I know who stands behind.
> The God of Angel Armies
> is always by my side.
>
> The one who reigns forever;
> He is a friend of mine.
> The God of angel armies
> is always by side."

I lost it, as uncontrollable tears streamed down my face. My friend looked at him and said, "Do you know who wrote and sings that song?" The pastor answered, "I have no idea." My friend said, "You're looking at him!"

The pastor grabbed me and hugged me so hard I could hardly breathe. Now he was crying as he said, "You have no idea what this song means to me. This is my song of faith." Crying now, I had no words. The pastor grabbed his phone and with laughter said, "Would you like to hear your song in Arabic?" I exclaimed, "Of course I would!" He said, "It's the only song on my phone." He pushed play and there it was, "God of Angel Armies," the familiar melody in the language of a foreign land. I can only hope to someday meet the Arabic artist who sang the song. He nailed it.

I'll never sing that song again without thinking of this Syrian pastor, a stunning portrait of the worship-led life. To this day, I hold him close in my heart.

THE BRIDGE

I'm wondering about you today. Do you find yourself in a storm, in a pit of despair, seemingly struggling alone and feeling desperate—gripped by fear? I want us to rebuke the fear and realign with the faith of a worship-led life. I want you to eat this word from the Man of God, the prophet Elisha:

> *"Don't be afraid," the prophet answered. "Those who are with us are more than those who are with them."*
> 2 Kings 6:16

Now I want you to drink in this word from the beloved disciple, John:

> *You, dear children, are from God and have overcome them, because the one who is in you is greater than the one who is in the world.* 1 John 4:4

SING WITH ME

Can you guess what song we are going to sing today? Yep! Dial up "God of Angel Armies." We will give it all we've got. And let's sing it as a blessing over the names and faces Jesus brings to our minds. Then let's also invite Bethel to lead us today in their powerful song "Goodness of God."

HOW GREAT?

How is your faith growing in the awareness of what God is doing behind the thin veil of apparent reality, on the other side of what you can see with your eyes? How are you taking tangible steps to live a secret life of faith before God and a hidden life of extravagant love for others?

I Will Follow

I wrote a song a few years back called "I Will Follow." The chorus captures the worship-led life. At the time I thought the chorus was pretty catchy. Even today I find myself singing it on a regular basis—a kind of prayerful declaration. You may remember it:

Where You go, I'll go
Where You stay, I'll stay
When You move, I'll move
I will follow You
Who You love, I'll love
How You serve I'll serve
If this life I lose, I will follow You
I will follow You

That's the storyline of the Bible, isn't it? Person after person, from Abraham to Esther and from Elijah to Mary, these are the ones who show us the worship-led life. If you want to see a highlight reel, check out the eleventh chapter of Hebrews. Here's a highlight:

> By faith Abraham, when called to go to a place he would later receive as his inheritance, obeyed and went, even though he did not know where he was going. By faith he made his home in the promised land like a stranger in a foreign country; he lived in tents, as did Isaac and Jacob, who were heirs with him of the same promise. For he was looking forward to the city with foundations, whose architect and builder is God.
> Hebrews 11:8–10

That's what I want them to say about us: "They were looking forward to the city with foundations, whose architect and builder is God." By far, though, my favorite line is: "He lived in tents." Abraham didn't take a mission trip. He lived a mission life. He left it all on the field.

Have you ever met someone and thought, *If the Bible were being written right now, this person would be in it.* I had the honor to meet such a man, Charles Mulli, and hear his story. Mully (as he is called) told me he grew up as an orphan in Kenya, living on the streets for years, in the soul-crushing condition of feeling unwanted. He would go door to door asking for help and was completely ignored until an Indian woman took him in. She not only gave him food and shelter but also introduced him to the love and grace of God.

Mully worked hard, developed a knack for business, and went on to build a real estate and oil empire in Kenya. He rose to become highly respected and revered as one of the wealthiest persons in the nation, accumulating many homes and a staff of servants along the way. I was stunned as he recounted to me his apostle Paul–like Damascus Road experience. Jesus turned his life upside down. Then Mully knew what he had to do. God was asking him to lay it all down. The assignment involved laying down the businesses he had worked so hard to build and lifting up the children who now lived in the place from which he had come—the streets. He said to me, "Everyone thought I had lost my mind, including my family."

Wasting no time, Mully began bringing children into his family's home. He would go out night after night into the darkness of the city, searching for children who were abandoned and alone, sons and daughters relegated to sleeping in the streets. One by one, Mully would pick them up, put them in his arms, tell them they were safe and that all would be OK, and bring them home.

His wife, Esther, a saint in her own right, would find another place on the floor for the new child to sleep and add another plate to the table. Soon their home was bursting at the seams with children. And then Mully remembered the undeveloped property he had purchased in hopes of one day building his dream: a family compound. He knew that God wanted him to use it to start building shelter for children.

Did I mention the property was undeveloped—so much so that it had no running water? It was pretty much a desert. Undeterred, Mully continued building home structures, and the kids kept coming. Desperate for water, he called every oil drilling engineer he knew to come and help him find a place to dig a well. Time and time again, the answer was, "There's no water on this land."

Mully told me, "One night God woke me up and told me to start walking, and He would tell me where to stop and that would be the place to drill for water." He got up out of bed in the dead of night, grabbed a lantern, and just started walking. Sure enough, after a pretty good walk, he said he felt God tell him to stop. He made a mark on the dry, cracked ground.

The next day, Mully brought many workers and even more of the young men he had rescued out to the mark and told them about his revelation from God: "The water is here. Start digging." They dug for days on end but found no water. Mully must have felt like Noah. Still, he told them to keep digging. As you might imagine, to everyone but one man's surprise, they hit the water source. Mully showed me a picture of what the ground looked like before the water and what it looks like now.

Would you believe that this land is now one of the largest and most fruitful farms in all of Kenya? It honestly looks like how I would envision the Garden of Eden. From an absolute desert to a lush, fertile paradise filled with food and with a water source that won't stop. Mully went on to tell me miracle after miracle that continues to happen there to this very day.

There is a documentary of his life called *Mully*. I highly recommend it. More important than that, get involved with his mission and charity: mcfus.org. Mully is now famously known as having the largest family in the world. As I write this, he and Esther have personally rescued over twenty-six thousand children and currently care for over six thousand. Wow. Talk about a worship-led life. I want to be Mully when I grow up. The me-driven life would have for sure kept Charles and Esther Mully on the path of wealth and homes and easy-street retirement. But they are as beautiful a picture of worship-led lives as I have ever seen.

THE BRIDGE

Spend some time in Hebrews 11. It has been called the Hall of Faith, not to be confused with the me-driven world's Hall of Fame. Ponder this additional bit of the chapter:

> *People who say such things show that they are looking for a country of their own. If they had been thinking of the country they had left, they would have had opportunity to return. Instead, they were longing for a better country—a heavenly one. Therefore God is not ashamed to be called their God, for he has prepared a city for them.* Hebrews 11:14–16

Who in your life is one of these kinds of people? Take a minute today and let them know. Call or text or, even better, write an old-fashioned letter. It will matter to them—a lot.

SING WITH ME

Today let's sing "I Will Follow." And then endlessly repeat it: "Where you go, I'll go. Where you stay, I'll stay. When you move, I'll move. I will follow you."

HOW GREAT?

Are you ready to move beyond a mission trip orientation to a mission life way of being in the world? Are you learning the way of quick and even immediate obedience in response to the promptings of the Lord? How are you making yourself at home in the promises of God as they relate to your love for other people?

20

I Speak Jesus

In the second chapter of the Acts of the Apostles, we find the moving story of the Day of Pentecost. On this, the first day of the Church, we read of the gospel being preached in foreign languages by people who couldn't speak those languages, all accompanied by a mighty wind and tongues of fire. Three thousand souls became saints that day.

That was the first story of the Church, yet something different happened in the very next chapter—something super small and powerful.

Peter and John were walking down the street, headed to the temple for the three o'clock prayer time. They came to the gate known as the Beautiful Gate. Let's invite the Bible to narrate for us:

> *Now a man who was lame from birth was being carried to the temple gate called Beautiful, where he was put every day to beg from those going into the temple courts.* Acts 3:2

Can you believe this? They carried this man to the gate of the house of God every day so he could beg from church people.

When he saw Peter and John about to enter, he asked them for money. Acts 3:3

So far everything is happening on cue. It's the predictable cycle of charity. Then this:

Peter looked straight at him, as did John. Then Peter said, "Look at us!" Acts 3:4

Peter wanted this man to see something different than the predictable cycle of charity; he wanted him to behold the face of love.

So the man gave them his attention, expecting to get something from them. Acts 3:5

The outward movement of Jesus is never transactional. It's always relational. Every single day, every single person we meet is an unrepeatable miracle of God. No matter how challenging the circumstances or difficult the hand life has dealt them, they are an image bearer of Almighty God. I hate it when people are defined as "needy" or "underprivileged" or put in some kind of category according to their problem. They are a human being, just like you and me. Peter and John engage this man not at the point of his need but at the heart of his humanity. Watch what unfolds:

Then Peter said, "Silver or gold I do not have, but what I do have I give you. In the name of Jesus Christ of Nazareth, walk." Acts 3:6

Peter and John knew that the Spirit of the Sovereign Lord was upon them. They trusted the Spirit's anointing. They took the risk of faith and moved in the name of love. That name is Jesus.

Taking him by the right hand, he helped him up, and instantly the man's feet and ankles became strong. He jumped to his feet and began to walk. Then he went with them into the temple courts, walking and jumping, and praising God. Acts 3:7–8

The story began with "a man who was lame from birth" and ended with "walking and jumping, and praising God."

A song I love called "I Speak Jesus" was written by a group of worship leaders who work under the collective name Here Be Lions. A member of this collective, Jesse Reeves, is one of my longtime friends—he played bass guitar with my band for decades and also helped write some of our best songs (including our title track, "How Great Is Our God"). One day Jesse prayed over this songwriters' collective as they gathered for a writing session, and his prayer became a song:

I just wanna speak the name of Jesus
Over every heart and every mind
'Cause I know there is peace within Your presence
I speak Jesus

I just wanna speak the name of Jesus
'Til every dark addiction starts to break
Declaring there is hope and there is freedom
I speak Jesus

Isn't this exactly what happened at the gate called Beautiful on the day after Pentecost? Peter spoke the name of Jesus over the broken man: "Silver or gold I do not have, but what I do have I give you. In the name of Jesus Christ of Nazareth, walk."

The song catches fire with the chorus:

'Cause Your name is power
Your name is healing
Your name is life
Break every stronghold
Shine through the shadows
Burn like a fire.

The great need of our time is not for more charity. It is for more Jesus. All the silver and gold in the world can't solve the problems of our time. Only Jesus can. And He has decided to do it through us. Said another way, He will not do it without us. What would it look like for a generation to become fluent in the language of speaking Jesus?

A day is coming, indeed has already begun, when every person who has ever lived will speak the name of Jesus. I love how the apostle Paul spoke of this coming day:

Therefore God exalted him to the highest place and gave him the name that is above every name, that at the name of Jesus every knee should bow, in heaven and on earth and under the earth, and every tongue acknowledge that Jesus Christ is Lord, to the glory of God the Father. Philippians 2:9–11

THE BRIDGE

I especially love the bridge of this song:

> Shout Jesus from the mountains
> Jesus in the streets
> Jesus in the darkness over every enemy
> Jesus for my family
> I speak the holy name
> Jesus

SING WITH ME

Let's sing this riveting and stirring song we've been talking about today, "I Speak Jesus." It's in the playlist (www.christomlin.com/singwithme).

HOW GREAT?

If "speaking Jesus" were a language, how are you becoming more fluent in speaking this language? How are you learning to "speak Jesus" over your family, your friends, even your enemies? How about over your neighbors and neighborhood? How about over your city? How about over conflicts and wars among nations? How are your prayers leading your feet into action?

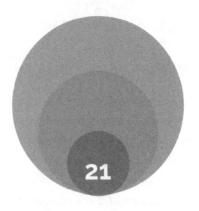

Midnight Worship

A s we turn toward home and the close of this letter-like volume of reflections from me to you, we need to level set around the bottom line. The worship-led life is not an easy life. It reminds me of how Paul and Silas were severely beaten, thrown in a prison cell, and chained to the floor—and all this for setting free a woman who had been trafficked into slavery. Behold, now, what a worship-led life looks like at midnight from jail:

> *About midnight Paul and Silas were praying and singing hymns to God, and the other prisoners were listening to them.* Acts 16:25

I call this the worship of midnight. Paul knew it well, as does anyone who persists in a worship-led life. Here's how he put it:

> *We are hard pressed on every side, but not crushed; perplexed, but not in despair; persecuted, but*

not abandoned; struck down, but not destroyed.
2 Corinthians 4:8–9

Later in his letter he would pull back the veil and show us his wounds:

Five times I received from the Jews the forty lashes minus one. Three times I was beaten with rods, once I was pelted with stones, three times I was shipwrecked, I spent a night and a day in the open sea, I have been constantly on the move. I have been in danger from rivers, in danger from bandits, in danger from my fellow Jews, in danger from Gentiles; in danger in the city, in danger in the country, in danger at sea; and in danger from false believers. I have labored and toiled and have often gone without sleep; I have known hunger and thirst and have often gone without food; I have been cold and naked. 2 Corinthians 11:24–27

I learned recently how the word *vulnerable* comes from the Latin word *vulne,* which means "to show the wounds." That reminds me of the third verse from the great hymn "Crown Him with Many Crowns":

Crown him the Lord of love;
behold his hands and side,
rich wounds, yet visible above,
in beauty glorified

Do you see this? He still bears the wounds. They are transformed now—in beauty glorified—as the scars of glory. The wounds of the cross are real, and though Jesus bears them, we carry them. That's what it means to "take up our cross" every day. We carry the wounds of Jesus in our very body. Paul continued:

We always carry around in our body the death of Jesus, so that the life of Jesus may also be revealed in our body. 2 Corinthians 4:10

The difference between a worship-led life and life in the me-driven world is not the presence of suffering, hardship, difficulty, and loss. It is in how Jesus takes up these things and transforms them into scars of glory. Look at how Paul put it:

For we who are alive are always being given over to death for Jesus' sake, so that his life may also be revealed in our mortal body. So then, death is at work in us, but life is at work in you. 2 Corinthians 4:11–12

I have been privileged to behold a few men and women who chose the worship of midnight—to worship in the midst of the worst pain and suffering in this life. I'll never forget hearing the news in 2008 of my dear friend and music hero, Steven Curtis Chapman, losing his five-year-old daughter to a freak accident at their home. Watching him and Mary Beth and the whole family walk through the darkest night of the soul has been heartbreaking and powerful all at the same time. A few years back, I was visiting Steven at his house. He shared with me how instead of moving away from the scene of the accident, they chose to stay and declare heaven's victory and God's goodness over the pain of death. He showed me a picture of the family standing in front of a wall at their house, boldly spray-painted with these words: "The enemy's been defeated."

I saw the same response in my friends Amanda and Toby McKeehan, aka "Toby Mac." We gathered under a massive oak tree to celebrate and mourn the tragic death of their firstborn son, Truett. Surrounded by a large crowd, drowning in an ocean of tears, we beheld the lifted hands of Toby and Amanda—midnight worship. My friend Matt Redman, no stranger to the worship of midnight, put it this way in his timeless song:

> Blessed be Your name
> On the road marked with suffering
> Though there's pain in the offering
> Blessed be Your name

Louie Giglio, founder of Passion and more movements in the Kingdom of Jesus than anyone will ever know, has taught me more about the worship-led life than anyone else. He and I wrote a song some years ago to help lead the Church in the darkest hours of midnight worship. Here's a bit of it:

> There's a peace I've come to know
> Though my heart and flesh may fail
> There's an anchor for my soul
> I can say "It is well"
>
> Jesus has overcome
> And the grave is overwhelmed
> The victory is won
> He is risen from the dead

And I will rise when He calls my name
No more sorrow, no more pain
I will rise on eagles' wings
Before my God fall on my knees
And rise
I will rise

That's the worship of midnight, my friends—the worship-led life both at its hardest and its finest. And let's not forget what happened in that dank prison cell with which we began today. As Paul and Silas were singing out their midnight songs of worship to God—this happened:

Suddenly there was such a violent earthquake that the foundations of the prison were shaken. At once all the prison doors flew open, and everyone's chains came loose. Acts 16:26

Here's how Paul summed it all up:

It is written: "I believed; therefore I have spoken." Since we have that same spirit of faith, we also believe and therefore speak, because we know that the one who raised the Lord Jesus from the dead will also raise us with Jesus and present us with you to himself. 2 Corinthians 4:13–14

But my favorite part of "I Will Rise" is the bridge. As Louie and I wrote the song, we envisioned scenes like the Chapman and McKeehan families grieving at gravesites, as the song of heaven broke through the skies:

And I hear the voice of many angels sing,

"Worthy is the Lamb"
And I hear the cry of every longing heart,
"Worthy is the Lamb"

Can you hear it? It's the everlasting song of the worship-led life. Will you sing with me?

THE BRIDGE

Someone once told me there are two kinds of people in this world: people who are going through hard times and people who are about to be. Take heart, my friends, and be of good courage. Jesus wins. Walk on the bridge of these words Paul wrote to close out the chapter we have traversed today:

> *Therefore we do not lose heart. Though outwardly we are wasting away, yet inwardly we are being renewed day by day. For our light and momentary troubles are achieving for us an eternal glory that far outweighs them all. So we fix our eyes not on what is seen, but on what is unseen, since what is seen is temporary, but what is unseen is eternal.* 2 Corinthians 4:16–18

SING WITH ME

We must sing "I Will Rise" together today. Gather up in your heart all those you know right now who are living in a season of midnight worship. As we sing, lift them up in prayer through this song. Let's also sing Matt Redman's song we rehearsed earlier, "Blessed Be Your Name."

HOW GREAT?

Did any stories of "midnight worship" come to mind as you read through today's entry? Have you ever publicly shared this story? Would you ever consider sharing it? What people in your life and sphere of influence come to mind who may be living in a midnight worship situation just now? How might you encourage them today?

BENEDICTION

A few years back I had the honor of leading worship at the Tennessee Prayer Breakfast hosted by the governor. Alongside me was Country Music Hall of Fame songwriter Tom Douglas. Tom was the co-writer of one of my favorite country music songs of all time, "The House That Built Me." Tom said something that morning that I'm still thinking about years later: "All of my songs, in the end, are really about home. Home is the great four-letter word. Everyone is either running from it or running to it."

Home is a place where we have all been hurt and yet home is the only place where we can ultimately be healed. It's our deepest longing, isn't it, to be at home and belong?

Jesus had a thing or two to say about home. Here's one of my favorites:

> *Anyone who loves me will obey my teaching. My Father will love them, and we will come to them and make our home with them.* John 14:23

We will make our home with them. This is where the worship-led life is always leading—home. Here's the mystery. Because of the presence of God with us, we are always home and yet we are always going home. Earlier in this same conversation, Jesus said this:

> *Do not let your hearts be troubled. You believe in God; believe also in me. My Father's house has many rooms; if that were not so, would I have told you that I am going there to prepare a place for you? And if I go and prepare a place for you, I will come back and take you to be with me that you also may be where I am.* John 14:1–3

We've all heard the sentimental saying, "Home is where the heart is." It's not true, is it? Here's the truth: home is where our God is. This world is the only home we know, and yet this world is not our home. Our home is with God, and God's home is with us. Still, we find ourselves living in an in-between place, don't we? We are at home because God is dwelling in us, and yet we still find ourselves in such a broken world, which leaves our hearts longing for a better city, as the Scriptures say, "the city with foundations, whose architect and builder is God" (Hebrews 11:10).

I was blessed to record the prolific song "Is He Worthy?" written by Andrew Peterson and Ben Shive. Through a call and response structure, the song profoundly captures both the brokenness and the beauty of this longing for home and draws the Church to dwell deeply within it:

Do you feel the world is broken?
We do.

Do you feel the shadows deepen?
We do.
But do you know that all the dark won't stop the
    light from getting through?
We do.
Do you wish that you could see it all made new?
We do.

Is all creation groaning?
It is.
Is a new creation coming?
It is.
Is the glory of the Lord to be the light within our
    midst?
It is.
Is it good that we remind ourselves of this?
It is.

The worship-led life cries out for more songs like this one, pairing the painful honesty of *what is* with the glorious realism of *what will be*. It's why Ed Cash and I wrote a song called "Home":

This world is not what it was meant to be
all this pain, all this suffering
but there's a better place waiting for me in heaven

every tear will be wiped away
every sorrow and sin erased

we dance on seas of amazing grace in heaven

I'm going home
where the streets are golden, every chain is broken
Home
where every fear is gone, I'm in your open arms
where I belong
Home

I was blessed to become friends with a man named
Blessing Offor after finding a demo of a song he had written. His story blew me away. Born in Lagos, Nigeria, Blessing lost his vision as a six-year-old. He wrote that song,
"Tin Roof," about his longing for heaven, based on the
deepest memory of his childhood home. He told me: "It
was the sound of the heavy rains falling loudly on the tin
roof of our home that conveyed to me the deepest safety of
home. I knew this must be what heaven is like." With the
help of songwriter Natalie Hemby, Blessing brought forth a
song of eternity for our time:

> Maybe the streets are gold and there's a table with
>   plenty room
> Maybe we don't grow old and we got nothing
>   to lose
> Maybe in the promised land, there's a choir when
>   you walk through
>
> Oh, but I pray Heaven is like rain on a tin roof
>
> Maybe the sun don't set and the waters don't rise
> Maybe we don't forget how to laugh like a child

Maybe in the promised land, we're all made for
    what we do

Oh, but I pray Heaven is like rain on a tin roof

Washing away
Washing away my sorrows
Giving me faith
Giving me faith to follow
A new tomorrow
They tell me in the promised land
There are mansions to choose

Oh, but I pray Heaven is like rain on a tin roof

Maybe time stands still and the mountains just move
Maybe we all have wings and there's only good
    news, oh
They say the living water is the fountain of youth

Oh, but I pray Heaven is like rain on a tin roof

The apostle Paul wrote, "to live is Christ and to die is gain" (Philippians 1:21) and also that he would prefer "to be absent from the body, and to be present with the Lord" (2 Corinthians 5:8 KJV). Yes, when we breathe our last, we will be instantly at home in the Lord's presence. Be clear, though: absence from the body is still not the end and final home. Hear Paul out:

> Listen, I tell you a mystery: We will not all sleep, but we will all be changed—in a flash, in the twinkling of an eye, at the last trumpet. For the trumpet will

sound, the dead will be raised imperishable, and we will be changed. 1 Corinthians 15:51–52

At the end of all things broken and the beginning of all things made new, we will behold the new heavens and the new earth. Home will come to us. The Bible says it best:

Then I saw "a new heaven and a new earth," for the first heaven and the first earth had passed away, and there was no longer any sea. I saw the Holy City, the new Jerusalem, coming down out of heaven from God, prepared as a bride beautifully dressed for her husband. And I heard a loud voice from the throne saying, "Look! God's dwelling place is now among the people, and he will dwell with them. They will be his people, and God himself will be with them and be their God. 'He will wipe every tear from their eyes. There will be no more death' or mourning or crying or pain, for the old order of things has passed away."

He who was seated on the throne said, "I am making everything new!" Then he said, "Write this down, for these words are trustworthy and true." Revelation 21:1–5

There's an ancient song called the "Gloria Patri" that brings it all together.

Glory be to the Father;
and to the Son, and to the Holy Ghost;
as it was in the beginning,
is now, and ever shall be,
world without end. Amen, amen.

The worship-led life takes us from sin and death to salvation and life, and all within the much larger story of creation to new creation and from all things broken to all things made new.

That, my friends, is the bridge of all bridges. Now sing with me . . .

A thousand generations falling down in worship
To sing the song of ages to the Lamb
And all who've gone before us and
    all who will believe
Will sing the song of ages to the Lamb
Your name is the highest
Your name is the greatest
Your name stands above them all
All thrones and dominions
All powers and positions
Your name stands above them all

And the angels cry: Holy!
All creation cries: Holy!
You are lifted high: Holy!
Holy Forever!

Hear your people sing, Holy
To the King of Kings, Holy
You will always be, Holy
Holy forever!

AFTERWORD

'
ve never been great at math. I remember arriving at college and basically having to start over in "developmental" math. I do appreciate data and statistics. A few years ago, a particular statistic grabbed my attention like no other: the number of kids who are booted out of their homes, living in a kind of forced exile. They have either left or been removed from their homes because of neglect, abuse, or otherwise intolerable living conditions. Does anyone want to guess the number of children facing those conditions?

Appoximately 400,000.

Those 400,000 children now live in what we call the foster care system. They live in someone else's home as a temporary holding place. The average child in this system is passed around to seven different homes before being reunited with their family of origin. For good reasons, many of these children never return to their biological parents. They wait day after day, month after month, year after year for an adoptive family. Whether they are reunited or end up on the adoption path, kids impacted by foster care across the United States long for the stability so many of us take for granted: a safe, secure, stable, loving family and home. Today, there are only about 200,000 foster homes across the country. This is a scary gap, and it means there are just not enough ideal homes to care for kids with complex needs.

There is another statistic I find compelling. Would anyone care to guess the number of local churches in the United States of America?

Approximately 350,000.

TODAY: 400,000 children exiled from their homes and in the foster care system. TODAY: 200,000 foster homes available. TODAY: 350,000 local churches (with many millions of families).

These children are not homeless. It's worse than that: in the worst moment of their lives, they are far too often family-less. We should be thankful for the thousands of families who are already standing in the gap in heroic fashion. But many, many foster children will never return to their families and spend years waiting for adoption into a forever home. It seems like it should be a short putt to close the gap if we organized an effort to invite the Body of Christ from among our 350,000 churches to step forward and *proclaim good news* to the 400,000 children in foster care saying, "*Your childhood will not be oppressed. We long for you to be set free.*"

One of my friends who works day in and day out to meet this challenge said this to me recently, "What if we change the waiting list? What if, instead of a list of children waiting for a safe, loving, ideal home, we had a list of families waiting and ready to serve?" I think about this all the time.

Because this is what happens when a kid reaches 18 and ages out of the foster care system without having been adopted:

Approximately 50 percent end up in chronic poverty.

Aproximately 90 percent risk being involved in the criminal legal system (when they have been moved to 5 or more placements).

Approximately 71 percent of young women are pregnant by 21 years old.

Approximately 40 percent will be homeless within 18 months.

Approximately 20 percent are homeless the day foster care ends.

This is the story of TODAY.

After that sobering note, permit me to close with the story of TOMORROW, in Jesus's words:

> *"When the Son of Man comes in his glory, and all the angels with him, he will sit on his glorious throne. All the nations will be gathered before him, and he will separate the people one from another as a shepherd separates the sheep from the goats. He will put the sheep on his right and the goats on his left.*
>
> *"Then the King will say to those on his right, 'Come, you who are blessed by my Father; take your inheritance, the kingdom prepared for you since the creation of the world. For I was hungry and you gave me something to eat, I was thirsty and you gave me something to drink, I was a stranger and you invited me in, I needed clothes and you clothed me, I was*

sick and you looked after me, I was in prison and you came to visit me.'

"*Then the righteous will answer him, 'Lord, when did we see you hungry and feed you, or thirsty and give you something to drink? When did we see you a stranger and invite you in, or needing clothes and clothe you? When did we see you sick or in prison and go to visit you?'*

"*The King will reply, 'Truly I tell you, whatever you did for one of the least of these brothers and sisters of mine, you did for me.'*" Matthew 25:31-40

Do we need a reminder of what He will say to those on his left?

It's still *today*.

Will you join me in praying for thenumber of children without families to continue to lessen until it is zero? And will you pray to become part of the solution—perhaps only in your prayers but possibly as part of the answer? We can do more than pray but we will never do more than pray until we have prayed. Will you pray with me for local churches and the millions of families they represent to wake up to the possibility of being part of the answer to this prayer?

In your praying, will you add this word from Isaiah, turned red letters by Jesus: "*Today* this scripture is fulfilled in your hearing." Declare it with boldness over every situation of need the Lord brings across your path.

ACKNOWLEDGMENTS

FROM CHRIS TOMLIN

It takes a great team to do anything worthwhile. I have had the privilege of wind in the sails from so many along the journey of my music career. Without them, my little boat would have never left the dock. Though I carry a lifetime of acknowledgements for a book like this, here are some friends and family that helped me get this one to the finish line.

J.D. Walt . . . my longtime friend, a humble giant of the faith—for diving into this endeavor with me and helping me create and craft these pages. You have a brilliant mind and pen.

EMF Publishing team—Dave Schroeder, Jenaye Merida, David Pierce . . . for believing wholeheartedly in the idea of this book.

Piedmonte & Co.—Anthony and Mak for continually pouring your lives into this mission with me of giving people a voice to worship God.

Capitol CMG team—Brad, Hudson, Sly, . . . for your continued belief and patience over two decades of making music together.

Curtis & Co.—Richard and team for keeping me on the rails.

Lauren—I love you with all my heart and am forever grateful to God for you . . . a constant source of strength, my best friend.

Ashlyn, Madison and Elle—you three make me so proud to be your dad.

You the reader—in all the worlds of books, that you would entrust me enough to pick this one up and open these pages . . . I pray you are reminded of God's greatness and His grace yet again.

And ultimately, to God . . . when I grabbed my guitar that one morning and began singing out that simple chorus, "how great is our God," I had no idea the journey that would unfold. But with every breath, those words will always be my anthem!

FROM J. D. WALT

I'll never forget the first time I met Chris Tomlin. It was the late 1990s. Chris had come to be the worship leader at the church where I had just been hired as one of the pastors. Though we didn't know each other at all, we had been hired to give birth to a worshipping community called "The Harvest" within a larger church. My first meeting with Chris happened in the context of a rehearsal he was leading for the first Sunday of our new service. I knew immediately I was in the presence of a worship leader the likes of which I had never seen before. There was something about his presence, even in this rehearsal, that seemed to elevate and amplify the presence of God like nothing I had never experienced. Chris had this Spirit-assisted gift to be able to stand at the center of the stage and seemingly disappear into the throng of worshippers as the greatness of God filled the house.

In retrospect, I now recognize what I was witnessing in those early days. Chris was living a worship-led life. You see, these days so long ago were the days before Chris Tomlin had become the Chris Tomlin we all know. And the truth is, after all the records and recording milestones, the countless awards and accolades, and becoming the most sung songwriter in history, he's still the same Chris Tomlin he was before it all started. As we have grown our friendship over these years, I am more convinced today than I was on that first day—he's the real deal. On stage, off stage, backstage, and no stage, Chris lives a worship-led life from which has come lyrics and melodies that have and continue to lead generations in worship. I am grateful for the honor of being part of this little book, and I wanted to make this acknowledgement as a way of honoring Chris. His life and his legacy will forever sing, "How Great Is Our God." Thank you, my friend, for the invitation—as you put it so well—to "sing with me."

ABOUT THE AUTHORS

Chris Tomlin is a husband, father, and renowned worship leader. Heralded as the "most often sung artist in the world" according to *TIME* magazine, Tomlin has dedicated his life to his personal mission, to help give people a voice to worship God.

John David (J. D.) Walt is the pastor of Gillett Methodist Church in Gillett, Arkansas. He is the Founder and Sower-in-Chief of Seedbed, Inc. whose mission is to gather, connect, and resource the people of God to sow for a great awakening. Prior to Seedbed, he served as Vice President and Dean of Chapel at Asbury Theological Seminary. A speaker and conference leader, the author of a growing collection of books, and a songwriter, J. D. has mentored pastors and worship leaders around the world both well-known and unknown. He writes every day for the Seedbed Wake-Up Call, a daily meeting with Jesus followed by tens of thousands of readers.

REFERENCES

Anonymous, "Gloria Patri," (2nd Cent.), Public Domain.

Anonymous, "O Gladsome Light," (Phos Hilaron), Public Domain.

Aaron Boyd, Peter Comfort, Richard Bleakley, Peter Kernaghan, Andrew McCann, Ian Jordan, "God of This City," Copyright © 2008 Thankyou Music Ltd (PRS) worshiptogether.com Songs (ASCAP) sixsteps Music (ASCAP) All rights reserved. Used by permission.

Matthew Bridges (1851), Godfrey Thring (1871), "Crown Him with Many Crowns," Public Domain.

Ed Cash, Scott Cash, "Nobody Loves Me Like You," Copyright © 2018 S.D.G. Publishing (BMI) McTyeire Music (BMI) Capitol CMG Paragon (BMI) All rights reserved. Used by permission.

Scott Cash, Chris Tomlin, Ed Cash, "Whom Shall I Fear (God of Angel Armies)," Copyright © 2013 McTyeire Music (BMI) Twelve Lions Music (BMI) Worship Together Music (BMI) Capitol CMG Paragon (BMI) S.D.G. Publishing (BMI) All rights reserved. Used by permission.

David Crowder, Louie Giglio, Chris Tomlin, "Joyous Light, No One More Worthy," Copyright © 2004 Rising Springs Music (ASCAP) worshiptogether.com Songs (ASCAP) Vamos Publishing (ASCAP) All rights reserved. Used by permission.

Charity Gayle, "I Speak Jesus" Copyright © 2019 Integrity's Praise! Music (BMI), For Me and My House Songs (BMI).

Louie Giglio, Chris Tomlin, "Holy Is the Lord," Copyright © 2003 Rising Springs Music (ASCAP) worship together.com Songs (ASCAP) Vamos Publishing (ASCAP) All rights reserved. Used by permission.

Louie Giglio, Chris Tomlin, "Amazing Grace (My Chains are Gone)," Copyright © 2006 Rising Springs Music (ASCAP) worshiptogether.com Songs (ASCAP) Vamos Publishing (ASCAP) All rights reserved. Used by permission.

Louie Giglio, Jesse Reeves, Matt Maher, Chris Tomlin, "I Will Rise," Copyright © 2008 Thankyou Music Ltd (PRS) / Rising Springs Music (ASCAP) worship together.com Songs (ASCAP) Spiritandsong.Com Pub (BMI) Vamos Publishing (ASCAP) All rights reserved. Used by permission.

Keith Green, "O Lord, You're Beautiful," Copyright © 1980 Ears to Hear Music (ASCAP) All rights reserved. Used by permission.

Reginald Heber, "Holy, Holy, Holy, Lord God Almighty," 1826, Public Domain.

Jason Ingram, Matt Redman, Matt Maher, Chris Tomlin, "White Flag," Copyright © 2012 Thankyou Music Ltd (PRS)/Rising Springs Music (ASCAP) Twelve Lions Music (BMI) worshiptogether.com Songs (ASCAP) Worship Together Music (BMI) Valley of Songs Music (BMI) S.D.G. Publishing (BMI) All rights reserved. Used by permission.

Jason Ingram, Chris Tomlin, Reuben Morgan, "I Will Follow," Copyright © 2010SHOUT! Music Publishing (APRA)/Rising Springs Music (ASCAP) worship together.com Songs (ASCAP) Vamos Publishing (ASCAP) All rights reserved. Used by permission.

John Kelly, "Number of Youth in Formal Foster Care Continues to Decline, Imprint Survey Finds," The Imprint Youth and Family News, December 2023, https://imprintnews.org/youth-services-insider/fewer-foster-youth-homes-2023-imprint-survey-finds.

Richard Mullins, "I See You," Copyright © 1991 Universal Music—Brentwood Benson Publ. (ASCAP) All rights reserved. Used by permission.

John Newton, "Amazing Grace," 1779, Public Domain.

Blessing Offor, Natalie Hemby, "Tin Roof," Copyright © 2021 Vamos Publishing (ASCAP) Capitol CMG Genesis (ASCAP) All rights reserved. Used by permission.

Andrew Peterson, Ben Shive, "Is He Worthy?" Copyright © 2018 Junkbox Music (ASCAP) Vamos Publishing (ASCAP) Capitol CMG Genesis (ASCAP) All rights reserved. Used by permission.

Matt Redman, "The Heart of Worship," Copyright © 1997 Thankyou Music

Matt Redman, Beth Redman, "Blessed Be Your Name," Copyright © 2002 Thankyou Music Ltd (PRS) All rights reserved. Used by permission.

Jesse Reeves, Daniel Carson, Ed Cash, Chris Tomlin, "Jesus Messiah," Copyright © 2008 Rising Springs Music (ASCAP) worshiptogether.com Songs (ASCAP) Vamos Publishing (ASCAP) All rights reserved. Used by permission.

Jesse Reeves, Ed Cash, Chris Tomlin, "How Great Is Our God," Copyright © 2004 worshiptogether.com Songs/ sixsteps Music/ASCAP/Alletrop Music/BMI All rights reserved. Used by permission.

Jesse Reeves, J. D. Walt, Chris Tomlin, "The Wonderful Cross," Copyright © 2000 Rising Springs Music (ASCAP) worshiptogether.com Songs (ASCAP) Vamos Publishing (ASCAP) All rights reserved. Used by permission.

Laura Story, "Indescribable," Copyright © 2004 worship together.com Songs (ASCAP) sixsteps Music (ASCAP) Laura Story Music (ASCAP) All rights reserved. Used by permission.

Chris Tomlin, "We Fall Down," Copyright © 1998 Rising Springs Music (ASCAP) worshiptogether.com Songs (ASCAP) Vamos Publishing (ASCAP) All rights reserved. Used by permission.

Chris Tomlin, Scott Cash, Ed Cash, "Home," Copyright © 2016 S.D.G. Publishing (BMI) McTyeire Music (BMI)

Capitol CMG Paragon (BMI) All rights reserved. Used by permission.

Chris Tomlin, Jason Ingram, Phil Wickham, Brian Johnson, Jenn Johnson, "Holy Forever," Copyright © 2022 S.D.G. Publishing (BMI) Capitol CMG Paragon (BMI) All rights reserved. Used by permission.

Judson W. Van DeVenter, "I Surrender All," 1896, Public Domain.

Isaac Watts, "When I Survey the Wondrous Cross," 1707, Public Domain.

Rainer, Thom S., "Ten Major Trends for Local Churches in America," Church Answers, 2023, https://church answers.com/blog/ten-major-trends-for-local-churches -in-america-in-2023

Child Welfare, "National Foster Care Month," Key Facts and Statistics, Child Welfare.org, 2023, https://www .childwelfare.gov/fostercaremonth/awareness/facts/

Annie E Casey Foundation, "First-of-its-Kind Data Track Troubling Outcomes of Youth Transitioning to Foster Care," November 13, 2018, https://www.aecf.org /blog/first-of-its-kind-national-data-track-troubling -outcomes-of-youth-transitioning

RJ Leonard Foundation, "Teen Pregnancy and Foster Care," March 24, 2022, https://www.rjleonardfoundation.org /blog/teen-pregnancy-and-foster-care

The National Foster Youth Institute, "Housing and Homelessness," https://nfyi.org/issues/homelessness/

Charles Wesley, "Love Divine, All Loves Excelling," 1747, Public Domain.

STAY UP TO DATE ON MUSIC, TOURS AND MORE AT
CHRISTOMLIN.COM

Notes

Notes

Notes

Notes

Notes

Notes

Notes

Notes

Notes

Notes

Notes

Notes